Heliotrope & Hansie

Titles by this author

Chaya's Moonlight Mission
Heliotrope & Hansie

Heliotrope & Hansie

Bryan Williams

Borrowed
Lady Books

Copyright © Bryan Williams 2011

Bryan Williams has asserted his right under the Copyright, Designs and Patents Act, 1988, to be identified as the author of this work.

All rights reserved.
No part of this publication may be reproduced, stored in a retrieval system, or transmitted in any form or by any means, electronic, mechanical, photocopying, recording or otherwise, without prior written permission of the author.

ISBN 978-0-9560431-1-5

Printed and bound in the UK by
MPG Books Group, Bodmin and King's Lynn

First published in 2011 by

Borrowed Lady Books
31 Stevens Lane, Breaston, Derby, Derbyshire DE72 3BU

For my mother

Contents

Chapter 1	Mayday Colours	9
Chapter 2	A Dream Benefit Match	27
Chapter 3	Hansie And Grendel	47
Chapter 4	Canterbury Bells	61
Chapter 5	Bluer Than Oxalis	79
Chapter 6	Misadventure On A Bean-stalk	101
Chapter 7	The Tombeau De Miles	125
Chapter 8	Punter	155
Chapter 9	Lunch For The Projectionist	177

Chapter One

Mayday Colours

MAYDAY COLOURS
Yellow, blue, heliotrope, green
Were the Mayday colours of Garston girls,
Committed to Olive's memory, better
Than the teacher's. Arrayed in their dresses,
They formed a pattern—"Olive?"
"Yellow, blue, heliotrope, green."
The harmony was right. Then the matchworks.
Eye-brows burnt off, nine years' tedium;
But the memory of having a better
Memory than the teacher reminded her
That she was worth more than a job
In the matchworks. A son at university,
A daughter at university, a son
On the dole, straitened circumstances
When prosperity beckoned—yet constant
In Olive's memory were the four words
Which had been a badge for sixty years,
A reminder that she was special and relied on,
Yellow, blue, heliotrope, green.

—————

FRYSTON WOOD
My string is not so taut
As yesterday;
Nor do the shadows speak
So curiously;
Though the silver birches tremble
And leaves are a month away.

─────

Gower
In flower
In Sydney
Is not of the same kidney
As Boycott
Or even Walcott.

─────

They brought him frankincense
And myrrh;
Gold was not forgotten.
Did they think to make him
One of them, with frankincense
And myrrh?

─────

Bordeaux. And Richard, courtier
Red as bottled wine,
Disparaged from the tap,
Tells riddles on his beads.

─────

Mayday Colours

Your boots are red;
Your hair is brown;
Like a fallen leaf
You lie on my bed.

―――――

Had Pip gone with Estella
To Tarento for the sights,
Would they have danced the tarentella
Through the firefly-dotted nights?
Would they have bathed at midnight, trembling,
Lest the locals find alarming
Their unwonted English nakedness,
So comical and charming?

―――――

Why do you hide your hair in a wimple, Felicity?
Let its gold cascade gleam in my eyes,
Affording felicity.
Yet who could afford that gold,
    who could win that hand,
      win felicity?
She could shake many men with a shake of her hair,
Could Felicity.

―――――

I've never seen the Southern Cross
Nor gathered opals for myself.
I've never gazed in to Lake Titicaca.
Must I find opals in the play of feeling
About me, gaze in to eyes that are deep
As the roots of the Andes, deep

Heliotrope & Hansie

As the origins of pre-Incan
Civilisation? Here are my travels,
Here are my opals. Yet I yearn
For the Southern Cross.

─────

Did Sybilla make a syllabub for her jackaroo
And, when he sought her hand for her cooking, did she rue
That talent which enticed the wrong man to her, she
Who wished to feed men's minds with wit, scorning levity
As though it were a fraudulent claim of levitation?
She wanted society, not lonely lucubration.

─────

With crimson ooze from pulsing well
Keats wove his drowsy, dreamful spell.

Coleridge's pale lightning green
Flames against a goblin scene.

─────

RALPH TOUCHETT
Ralph loved without hope for himself, watching
Another's career as though he were hatching
Her from her American life, a chick
Who was destined to fly. The tick
Of a clock was more frequent for him,
Long-stricken, lung-stricken, eking out
His life by wintering in Tunis or Corfu
And dreaming of life where the air was fatal
For him, the air she breathed.

─────

Mayday Colours

PAKEEZAH
"I saw your angelic feet"
Went to her heart 'mid the smoke
Of Bradford, and her feet
Quickened to the rhythm
Of another life, a continent
Carried within her, precious
For the scowls of skinheads in the street,
Like an untouched Koh-i-noor.

─────

Sister of Alain-Fournier,
Daughter of Jacques Brel,
Huppert,
Adjani—
How these Isabelles follow me,
Prettier far than Elizabeth,
With the resonance
    of a chain of stones
On the neck
    of Marthe Keller's
Sanseverina.

─────

Azaleas, dogwood, Georgia pines,
Where golfers have manners as well as spines
And "gentle Ben" with "little Ben"
Caressing the ball to glory
On fiendishly undulating greens,
More treacherous than Fred Goodwin sands,
In a long curve, turning at right angles,
As a bridge is rounded in to perfection
By its ever-more-familiar underwater arch

Heliotrope & Hansie

In the golden Georgian sunlight
And magnolias, redolent of decay,
Take on another meaning from the "Masters".
Joseph had his coat of many colours
But Ben has his green jacket.

―――――

"M. Stendhal is working," reported Eugénie;
Forty years later,
The Prince Imperial dead in a foreign quarrel,
She sought the place of his death in darkest Africa,
Lost in undergrowth, yet she homed by instinct on to it,
Stood vigil all night long under strange stars.
How M. Stendhal would have appreciated the tale.

―――――

Adelaide, old-fashioned name, old-fashioned city,
What do you want with a motor-race?
When you are famed for fresh air and for pretty
Tree-lined avenues worthy of Baron Haussmann,
And your skies are as blue as a prophet's desert,
What do you want with a motor-race?

―――――

GARY COOPER
Whipcord elegance, taut as a bowstring,
Swifter than Legolas, surer tracking,
Able to twirl with the best of them,
Draw with the best of them, trade
Punches, parry wit, win
The most supercilious of women.
"Coop" was a gentleman of the wilds,

Mayday Colours

A Blondin mastering Niagara,
A lionheart with the graces of Charles 1.
Buckskin majesty, fitted for doeskin,
Scouting excessive compliment as well
As trails, bushman to outwit bushwhackers,
Ranger, who ranged to European culture,
Worldlywise beyond worldliness,
He found simplicity beyond the swamp.

―――――

'There was a photograph of Gary Cooper at the bus station — on an advertisement — and beside it: eternal flame." It had sent her with a smile through the shops and smiling home.

―――――

Will my jelly ever set?
My mother took the City and Guilds exam,
Passing the practical, failing the theory,
Was advised: "Catering's not for you, love,"
By a fellow-student, being slow and careful
And working her way towards an ideal recipe
Like Newton or Leonardo. Now I must
Feed myself, partly on fresh fruit, finding
Adroit, simple ways to toss off delicacies.
Will my jelly ever set?
Sprinkling cinnamon on dried apricots,
On Basmati rice — no saffron — I like
Saffron cakes when there is just enough
Saffron. I met the name in junior school:
'The Saffron Rover", a pirate ship,
Which turned out to be on the good side,
Freebooter for justice. Coffee is magical,
More magical than cinnamon when it's hot

Heliotrope & Hansie

Arabica, wafted upstairs on a sunny
Winter morning, like the scent of flowers
From Topol's oasis south west of the Dead
Sea. I may try a magnum opus, spicy
Fruit cake, with cane sugar—all important.
No base beet sugar ruining a lifetime's
Wisdom. But can I ever master food,
I who soaked up knowledge and forgot contacts,
Who proved himself impractical in England's eyes?
Can I triumph over England in my kitchen?
Will my jelly ever set?

─ ─ ─ ─ ─

'The joy of blue islands", the joy of green islands,
Warm so near the iceberg's path, refuge for crofters,
Haven for poets, more home than prison for all its small towns.
Louisbourg mastered, French only hired hands,
Indians far off in to the west.
Surplus of men out in to the west,
Calling Jane Andrews, plain, stupid Jane—
More plain than stupid?—to travel to the west,
Husband-hunting. She found one with money.
But what meant her money on a green island?
What means the joy of the greenest of islands,
Homeliest and most romantic of islands,
Home of the russet, home of the goldenrod,
Dells of activity amid the sleepiness?

─ ─ ─ ─ ─

Could Adjani be an adjunct to a man?
Would she mind? How easily she would bind
Him to her, nodded by her wayward head

Mayday Colours

To sleep in that Ophir of her bed
And regularly paint the night red
Or lilac.

—————

Oh, that I could lose
Myself in the hills about Toulouse.
There I'd find myself in the clear light
Of Mediterranean blues.
Far from the negro's black blues,
My heart would sing like Novalis.

—————

How strange to have German thoughts in your head,
To pour your subconscious through a different funnel,
As though you dreamed
Interplanetary colours.

—————

Is Trevor being pensioned off? I'll defend him motte and bailey,
Defend his right to wear the motley on his tongue,
Make a pal of Pagliacci, be indifferent to Versace,
Read about Biggles dodging archie,
Quaff a quick brandy in a crisis,
And pass on tips with exactingly good will.
My mother expected him to sound like Fred.
He did not defend like a toff with Willie Watson.
Indians knew him as "Stone-waller wallah".
A Bailey innings never came to the boil
But the bowler did—how he picked on Keith Miller.
His humour's not of the heads, though he be an ex-marine.
Doughty enough to have crossed Arabia, almost like crossing Lillee.

He's fond of Browning, that artful, underrated medium pacer
Of narrative verse, substantial in 'The Ring and the Book',
Graceful in the Campagna. My mother found him over-critical,
Then decided Fred had taken up his mantle.
But Yorkshire lugubrious is not Essex wry.
Trevor could move the ball and explain how,
Praising skill, shaking his head over shortcomings,
His comments terse and keen complementing the screen.

─────

Deep below the skyscrapers, Woody might have imagined himself in the pit of hell but, instead, felt comforted. 'They're very womblike, these buildings," he used to say, "and they symbolise powerful women. I feel like Gulliver with a sixty-foot Brobdingnagian girl when I look up. That's comforting. I feel protected. In Hollywood, they're Lilliputian. I'm afraid of treading on them. It worries me that I don't want to feel protective to a six-inch woman—the Bogart in me is challenged. My psychiatrist says I must have had a rocky love-life to equate women with concrete but he does say—and this fires me with a sense of having a role to play—I have an imaginative subconscious, ahead of its time, perhaps leading to the next stage of evolution. Or perhaps not. Still, he sees hope in my vision of George Gershwin tunes written on the concrete like black suspenders against the sunset. If I like George Gershwin, he says, there's more than concrete in my heart, only he prefers Jerome Kern and wonders if I've shied away from Jerome because of the Jerome Bible and instinctively gravitated towards George, seeing the world as full of dragons dead set against me. At least, he says, there's a sugary sort of concrete in my subconscious. I look up at buildings and see the women I have hang-ups about. He once asked me if I see myself as Aladdin, carrying the lamp of my pen and camera along these tunnels, with reality far above, a glimpse of blue between the roofs. No, I said. I've a secret fear that I'm the fall guy, Abanazer, some young guy is going to shine a lamp on me and I'm going to see I'm evil, Richard Nixon's conscience when his clinker hasn't been taken out and then some."

―――――

RADIO LEICESTER
Mike
     is handy with a mike
     and yet she'd like to spike
     his guns, his teasing humour.
Oh, this chaffing chafes my heart.
I'm not a singing chaffinch, a light-as-Lata
chaffinch, soaring, painting its soul on the
sky: it's my fourth programme.
Mike
     takes pity on his confreres—
What! A confrere in a sari? Consoeur, surely.
Mike
     thinks he spent another life stealing saris
à la Krishna.

―――――

Lost in the desert, Ben Elton began telling lavatory jokes to a lizard. It scuttled away disdainfully.

"How do you get a laugh out of a lizard?" Elton spoke aloud. His lips cracked. He needed an audience to keep him sane, to help him think—laughs were his cigarette. The sun was leaping up at him off the ground. He found another lizard lazing, playing doggo maybe in the hope that he would go away. He started again. If only there was some response. What would he have given for a rotten egg, a tomato? Dodging missiles, he could have felt at the sharp end of comedy, alive in a way he could never have been if he had followed in his family's academic footsteps, alive—for how long? His foul language was petering out in the desert air. It might have been the first grunts of primeval Man. Primeval—he liked the word, made a note to fit it in to his club act if he ever got out of here. What was it like to be the bleached bones of an explorer? With my audience, I was born-to be eaten by vultures, he thought. At least, explorers died going somewhere, knowing that Man had risen from primeval slime—he rolled it around his tongue like a pebble to moisten his mouth.

"How can you have a pebble in your mouth without swallowing it?" he thought. "That Demosthenes must have been a right twit. Did he have fifty-seven pebbles in his stomach?"

What if you were eaten by vultures when you weren't going anywhere? Elton saw his own bleached bones before him. "He told lavatory jokes and vultures ate him in the desert."

He found another lizard and began the second house.

"I'll go fishing. I'll take up golf. I'll try to write something that isn't empty." The lizard gave him a withering stare.

"I'll mend my ways. I'll try not to be loathsome." The sun was cooking him. He was hot stuff, Elton, especially now.

"Edwina Currie and Glenys Kinnock were in a sauna—and I'd even rather be there than here."

―――――

"Alf and Michael should duff up the scriptwriters," declared Ray Meagher. "I don't know whether we're friendly or feuding from one day to the next. You could be on your fanny or your feet. How long have they been mates? I can't for the life of me understand why they hate each other. At this rate, Don Fisher will turn out to be Alf's illegitimate elder brother, with a claim to the Stewart store, threatening to drive Alf to penury unless he goes in to partnership with Adam Cameron, fishing for pearls. I don't know who I am and who I like. I used to know where I stood with Alf. They even give me flamin's that aren't idiomatic. A bloke has a feel for these things after seven years."

'Too right," agreed Denis Coard. "If we were method actors—let's be method actors. Pirandello hits Summer Bay. Two actors in search of whatever number of scriptwriters we find are responsible."

―――――

"I had a wonderful cup of tea in the interval," said Michael Berkeley. "It's my lucky day—this morning a boiled egg knocked me out. Programmes at the Proms this year are like illuminated manuscripts—a joy to behold. Tonight, after the marvellous Finnish violin concerto, we have a superlatively original Szymanovski setting of the Stabat Mater and Scriabin wallowing in sensuality—a tremendous wallow—like a hippo, only better-looking. You can picture the pianist's head sinking beneath the mud, then, with a Lisztian toss of his leonine mane, with one bound, he's free. The spirituality of the Szymanovski and the sensuality of the Scriabin are... marvellously exciting, like alternate sips of iced champagne and hot coffee, only we haven't mixed them up—that would be really mind-blowing. It has been a privilege to be present at a concert of new music and old, superlatively played."
"Is there anything in your life that's mediocre?"

―――――

By Palumbo's reasoning, all artists who win prizes are no good. The Impressionists took a long time to win recognition, so no-one is allowed to question the talent of Palumbo's particular four avant-garde artists. What if people like other avant-garde artists? Are they still dunderheads and the art establishment, which is always wrong, right, being in the person of Palumbo?

―――――

Peter Palumbo pilloried was a great idea for performance art. He was hit in the face by eighty-nine custard pies, this being the chosen number for a pile of red bricks. Hieroglyphics were inscribed on every eleventh brick, Sumerian characters on every twenty-second and a bottle of champagne was smashed against the noble pile by Nicholas Serota. He then ate a symbolic rice pudding. Richard Cork went in to ecstasies about the project.

―――――

WHEN BLOFELD WAS ABSENT IN PERTH
Henry leave the flesh-pots of Sydney?
Henry go to the farthest west?
As soon swim the Bass Straits in his vest.
Not even beguiling cricket could wrest
Him away from his night-life. Oh, Henry,
"Martini" Henry, connoisseur of bikinis, Henry,
We need some puritanism in the box.
Many a time did Arlott go spare
And William Frindall tear his hair
But Blofeld went his burbling way
Whatever weather came his way,
Gaffes galore, Johnston without the scrupulous
Fairness, cakes without competence.
I sometimes feel that Cambridge rowers
Are no more partisan than Blowers;
But all-embracing bonhomie won tolerance.
I stopped switching him off.
The flowering of Blowers came after
His skull was cracked. Was he ever
The same again? Would the same
Have become famous? He's seldom lame
But often fatuous.

―――――

CAPE COD
She thought herself the bee's knees
As she took up keeping bees

Mayday Colours

In Devon, not exactly a seventh heaven
But a place of promise. No unleavened
Bread but cream teas would be their lot,
But she was Lot's wife, looked back
And was turned to a pillar of salt. More than a hack,
Less than a genius, Hughes writhed upon a rack
Of feminist hate while trying to transmute salt
To honey, the salty taste of the blood from the gaping wound
Her teeth left on his cheek, the salt spray of Cape Cod—
Could he make it Devon honey? Could he make
It honey for the world? She wrote of her father buried with a stake
Through his heart. She was the vampire on a Fulbright, licking her lips
As she thought of Cambridge and art and swift, violent men, brief, violent
Loves and a place in posterity.
You can't easily outfox a thoughtfox, even with your red brush—
Did he know her red brush when he wrote thoughtfox?
Was she red as her daughter's red or merely reddish?
Would she have called herself merely anything except mereweary?
The grapes of wrath, the words of Plath,
More angry than the grapes of wrath.
Intoxicated with destruction,
Galvanised with domestic ruction
As with electric shocks in the institution—
Was she saner for the shocks or madder for the shocks?
"Shucks! It's all one to me. I was lent
By my father's grave for a sojourn in letters,
Then back to the grave, wrenched open by poetry—
My pen is a crowbar, my images dynamite.
And what do I lever up? A robbed tomb.
Not even Boris Karloff lurking in the gloom.

———

Heliotrope & Hansie

Does Ginger warm Philip on a wintry walk
Or cool him in the Tube with a flashed
Remembered phrase across the talk,
Turning tunnels in to the grottoes
Of Capri? When boors barge him, flabby as Nero,
Does he picture Pyrrha's rincarnation
Slip past, sowing her perfume in his soul,
Brushing him with eternity? Once touched, ever touched,
As Horace sinks deeper year by year,
Making a schoolboy of the editor,
Even as he makes him wiser. Without Horace,
Where would Howard be? Without Pyrrha,
Where would Horace be? A flavour outlasts stone.

─────

I thought of Pyrrha in the Tube,
Pressed against a black "boob tube", With dreadlocks in my ears
And silver cigarette-case laughs
Braying from those less toffs than oafs
And chewing-gum stuck to my shoe—
Yet Pyrrha passed through my mind
And I felt enriched by that moment.

─────

Moongazer Meena saw her beauty in the moon,
Saw her loneliness in the moon.
Was she yellow, dancing,
White, alone?
Was her honeymoon a blue moon
Or was there never quite honey in her life?
Was it always just beyond her grasp, dancing,
Acting, living another's life more easily than her own?
Was her own heart, which finally struck her down, a stone?

Mayday Colours

Was wine, ever more wine, a milky way to float her high
In a night sky, a lonely loveliness?

―――――

Emma sings of coffee sweetly,
Flute following, sunniest of shadows,
And where, in Saxony's streets or meadows,
Was Bach inspired to set his notes so featly?
The dour old church composer unbends,
But, then, he never was a dour church composer,
Nor was he always old, and, even when old,
He skipped. His driving beat was not for the dozer.
From Leipzig to Formosa, he is known
For his dancing rhythms.

―――――

Why do you care for Katherine, Causley?
Why not Anne or Lady Jane?
Is it some other Katherine of England
You have in your muddled brain?
Or is it an unknown Katherine,
Another of Aragon,
You mourn in your naval solitude,
In love with your paragon?
It is many miles from Cornwall
To the Mediterranean seas
And it's hard to keep up comradeship
When you're grieving and on your knees
But there's one fancied Katherine of Aragon
Who breathes only in your verse
As Molière gave life to Harpagon.
Your love is as deep as terse.
There's naught you can do about submarines

Heliotrope & Hansie

Unless you can speed like the Queens,
And the mines of Golconda are not so deep
As the deep where mines will leave you to sleep;
But Causley has hours in which to reap
The harvest of thought before his watch.
Whose Katherine? Causley's Katherine, joyous in her early death,
Because she gives breath to the life that mourns
A comrade who crossed the last bourn.
He ties life and death in a true-love knot,
Sailor and queen, both sung, both loved, not
Forgotten.

Chapter Two

A Dream Benefit Match

A DREAM BENEFIT MATCH
"I'd better give you a few tips," said Shane Warne.

"You mean facts? I leave them to Gradgrind," retorted Dickens. "Cricket should be a joy. I played a little at school. I'll just turn my arm over as you do and inspiration will take over."

"If you want to bowl as I do, you need to know the grips and hand position for leg-break, wrong 'un, flipper, top-spinner, quick leg-break, wrong 'un with extra disguise, and the beauty Abdul Quadir taught me which deserves a special name."

"Would it destroy my creativity?"

'Tools of the trade," said Shane, bowling a leg-break. "Everyone knows, you make Thomas Kennealy look like a flat finger-spinner. You must have a rich vocabulary to do that, and a good general knowledge, and you must have learned English grammar."

"Young man, you're talking sense." Dickens warmed to his task. "Could you teach me a particularly deadly ball for George Eliot when she comes in with all her padding and that air of superiority because they think so much of her at Cambridge—you'd think she'd been to Cambridge herself?"

"Sounds like she could do with some sledging. We're whiter than white in that respect."

"I like the sound of this "flipper", and "wrong 'un" intrigues—does it describe a bent lawyer? Out of the common run of lawyers? You put me in Pickwick mood, taking the first steps in what, judging by the way that ball skidded through, is a noble and erudite calling.

Should I put my fingers in vinegar, so they'll have more strength and whip—prizefighters have pickled hands and head, I believe?"

"No need. You grow in to a leggie. Think of Richie Benaud. He has the look of a leggie. He knows about bowlers from way back, after your time but before mine. He could write a thesis on spin bowling, but he likes to keep it simple. I can't teach you everything straight away. Have a go and, at least, the batsman won't know what to expect."

"How do I get the batsman dithering?" asked Dickens.

"You could speak to the wicket-keeper. That gets them worried. Talk about the weather if you like, or try out a short story. Ian Healey likes a good yarn. Switch to round the wicket. They're terrified of the rough. Don't worry if you're hit for six. Pretend it's part of the plan."

'Talking of men after my time, will cold-hearted Evelyn Waugh be there?"

"I don't know about that, but Steve and Mark will be. D.H. Lawrence was in the nets. He called the late cut prissy."

"Worse than that," said Dickens. "While I was watching, he threw a drinks tray at David Gower and called him effete."

'The usual word is languid; careless when he gets out."

"Gower withdrew to the commentary box, saying: "Boycott hasn't thrown anything at me yet." Who's Boycott?"

"Some say he would bore the deepest oil well. I've met others who say he could play strokes when he felt like it. He's a Yorkshireman."

"Ah. Wackford Squeers country. After driving your friend, Gower, from the nets, Lawrence declared that the cross-bat hoik expresses the blood-knowledge of village blacksmiths stretching back to the first chestnut burr and Man's emergence, belly to ooze, belly to belly, belly to his destiny—he says the universe is in the belly."

"Someone's got a beer-gut."

"I believe in the spirit myself. We'd better keep Jane Austen away from him."

"No problem. She's scoring. She said she doesn't like to stray far

A Dream Benefit Match

from her writing-desk. We'll send McDermott in. Fast bowlers are built to take knocks. He can stand a few drinks trays from D.H. Lawrence. We'll tuck the Waughs away down the order until he's had a few drinks and is sleeping them off."

"Lawrence was always stamping on other people's pleasures. He wouldn't even let his wife wear pretty underclothes."

"Strewth!"

"Gower said someone called Beefy had insisted on going to court and lost—he can't have read "Bleak House"—to a marauding Pathan. I thought it was Hindus who objected to beef grease and Mussulmans to pig grease. That was what sparked off the Mutiny."

"I think Both objected to Imran and Imran to Both. The rest of us are glad we don't have to pay the lawyers' bills. Imran raided Australia a few years ago and took the World Cup."

'The North West Frontier come to New South Wales—the world has shrunk. Gower said Imran puts it about that he is descended from both Genghis Khan and Tamerlane so as to demoralise the opposition."

"I wasn't listening when we did them, but Genghis Khan would have thought twice about facing Denis Lillee. They say Denis believed a batsman who had been dropped three times had no right to be on the planet and he let him know that."

"I thought I was sending Micawber to an out-of-the-way spot, where he would be safe from turmoil, though I venture to suggest that he would have taken marauding Pathans at his most breezy, rather as he did kangaroos—or the voyage to Australia. I had to send Emily inland because she felt she must deny herself the pleasure of blue water, the dream of which had so beguiled her."

"You could have sent her to Tasy. Even at Palm Beach, the sea's not as blue as it's painted. Melbourne would have suited her. It can be bracing or steamy—makes us adaptable. You never get bored. They marvel at Melbourne weather in Sydney bars. It accounts for our solid character."

"Gower was talking to me about something called pyjama cricket. Is it caviar to the general or whelks to the gourmet?"

"Whelks, I think."

"We tried to persuade Kipling to play. He might have been very effective off a short run. He'll be reporting the match, with plenty of local colour and help about technique from Trevor Bailey."

"Gower suggested putting Andrew Marvell at silly point to give the batsman advice."

"He would do that admirably, but he can be belligerent. He might take his sword to the batsman."

"Tempting."

"But not cricket. I suppose there are regulations about side-arms in the field."

"No worries. Ian Chappell had a drink with him. They got on very well." "Marvell would bring all the colours of pyjamas in a harem to inquiries about the batsman's health, form, antecedents, political leanings, faith or lack of faith. He might do for the pitch what he did for the garden. I should have liked Richard Lovelace here, a noble soul but too fond of the bottle."

"I know a few like him."

"I don't say no to a bowl of punch after the match, but the excess of punch should be in the making of it, the slicing of lemons, the sprinkling of spices like a magician making a circle to shut out melancholy, the general revelry of festive cooking and festive serving and singing and merrymaking, a cinnamon stick a magic wand, a nutmeg a crystal ball to give us the aroma of the Indies at our own table. In drinking, there should be moderation if it is to be enjoyed. The opposition should be our nutmeg and we grate the confidence from them. Let the teams come together in fellowship after we have duly won our victory, grated them as though they were a nutmeg, sliced them like lemons, tickled them with a cinnamon stick and finally drowned them in punch."

"That's the spirit."

A Dream Benefit Match

After reading Dumas, I thought of Henri III as an effeminate weakling. In "La Reine Margot", he is big and brutal. Anjou is as much the driving force behind the massacre as the Guises. Charles IX, unhinged, orders the murder of his mentor, Coligny. Alencon is seventeen at the time. Henry of Navarre was in reality only nineteen. Is Margot's wedding-dress more gold than red? Charles bled on her white dress as La Mole had bled on her when she saved his life. Had she donned the white because it was Charles' favourite and she hoped to cajole him in to releasing La Mole? Margot smelt of jasmine when La Mole first made love to her. Cinq-Mars used to anoint himself with jasmine before going to see Louis XIII. Her blue eyes gleamed through a black mask, a carnival mask.

Henriette, her red-haired confidante, was apparently laughing as the Huguenots were massacred yet she came with six Catholic men to the aid of Margot and La Mole. Is she the one who is introduced as 'the Italian baroness" at the wedding festivities? Was it when alone with the ailing Charles that Margot wore two strands of pearls and pearls at her ears and in her hair? They gave her an Indian look.

The film takes a few minutes to gather momentum. Geoff Brown thought Isabelle was stiff in the wedding scene. Surely, it was written stiff. Playing a wanton, she did not exert herself. Her face turned at an angle and she flashed a characteristic smile. When Henri came to her bedchamber on their wedding night, Henry of Guise lurking in the shadows, eavesdropping, her eyes began to impose themselves on the screen. Theirs is the first intense scene. Henri said she would learn to drink wine and eat garlic in Navarre. Did she not in Paris? When Charlotte asked Henri to make love to her on his wedding night, Anjou had put her up to it.

Once the slaughter starts, Isabelle's eyes move amid chaos. She is the calm centre, the eye of the hurricane. Henri and Charles seek comfort in her and their mutual need for her draws them together. D. W. Griffith's tragic heroine of the massacre was called Brown Eyes; here blue eyes hold sway.

Her fingers hover over La Mole's severed head.

Invited to accompany her, Henriette declined, perhaps intending to return to Italy, so Margot lost friend as well as lover.

"Navarre awaits you," said her page. In the last moments of the film, the sun lit up her tresses.

─────

Niles was beaten to the hug.

"Should I abandon my karate lessons or is it worth working at training my body to seize the day?"

"Daphne, you mean?"

"Day, Daphne, come the four corners of the world in arms, I shall be ready."

"Niles, you're on the way up, but are you on the up and up?"

"I'm on the straight and narrow, the street called straight—is that in Damascus? I'm on the road to Damascus. I'm going to have a life that I never thought possible. Put out the flags. Hang Mans. Hang metaphors. What's a metaphor for but to serve—me, my country, my profession, the guild of lovers to which at last I aspire? Eureka! I've found Daphne and she's pure gold. Give me a bath and I'll leap from it. Give me somewhere to stand and I'll move the world. Someone's upset my chess-set and all my pieces are rolling on the floor, rolling in the hay like a rolling stone. I'm ahead of the fashion at last. I'm the voice of a generation. I'm babbling of green fields. I'm babbling of Starbuck's. Starbuck was on the Pequod and some who frequent Starbuck's would harpoon Moby Dick if they did but choose. Others may go to bars; I buck the trend, Starbuck the trend, put Starsky in his hutch, thumb my nose at the butch, I'm all over the heavens.

(In memory of David Angell, and with thanks to Peter Casey and David Lee)

─────

A Dream Benefit Match

Yellow was the Lutheran colour in southern France. It was worn with pride. When Henri reverted to the Protestant faith, a little girl held yellow flowers—the same colour as those at the foot of Isabelle's bath (and the colour of her silk curtains). Saffron is an aggressive colour to the B. J. P.; this is lighter, brighter, gentler. Some Protestants in the north, presumably Calvinist, wore black, which was considered provocative, as was their breaking windows and defacing of paintings in churches.

─────

Serge Lama described Françoise Hardy's first record as "so much against the fashion as to be almost mad, a romantic calm amid rock and James Deanism." In "Subway", Isabelle Adjani is a walking romantic calm, changing the mood whenever she comes on screen.

─────

Gabe was never an archangel, never sober-suited,
Never sobersides; he had not the spirit of Ironsides
Yet needed iron insides to cope with the drink.
Why did he dwell on synonyms for black when red tresses danced before his eyes and he saw a green sea, sober, and the last eyes he loved were brown? Was he getting ready for the dark, savouring the richness of black?
Why no red and why no white?
Why no river Shannon flowing?
You feel like Andrew Marvell mowing,
Save for the blackness that comes from knowing
Juliana came too late.
So many blacks and no cosmos.
Scent her universe with chocolate
Before you go the way of the Aztecs.

─────

If Turgenev said: 'There can be no art without patriotism.', it is incongruous because he lived outside Russia for many years, was very well-disposed towards Germans before the Franco-Prussian War, then started attacking Prussian militarism and died in the house of Pauline Viardot and her husband. "Smoke" expresses disillusionment with all parties in Russia. The old German music teacher in "On the Eve" has a boldness and power of imagination peculiar to German composers. Italian singers are expressive beyond other races. (I thought of Salvatore Adamo and Sinatra).

Isla came from the desert states
Over the sea to summer.
Can she act like Christopher Plummer?
Too much resting would be a bummer.
Can she find work with Dieter Brummer
Or only as a modern-day mummer
In some updated mystery play?
She could have found a rummer
Partner but one less of a bully
And aware of the cleaning up
Of water in Kazakhstan.

Almost black on Jane's white skin,
Valentine roses invite to sin.
Scentless roses she'd throw in the bin.

Like Richard II, she would give her jewels for a set of beads. Corals and seed pearls have long been close to her heart. Is she a votary of Coco Chanel?

A Dream Benefit Match

"Coffee's all very well, but give me Coco."

Fashion has gone from Coco Chanel to Coco the clown. String after string of beads, some priceless, some worthless, adorned her neck.

"I adore corals but I like another string to my bow." Pink or white? "I feel the fate of my bones against me. Shakespeare says I shall be coral. I'm adorned by my future."

"Would you rather be metamorphosed in to seed pearls?"

"Yes, if I could. Someone sympathetic could wear me to a ball and I could share a posthumous waltz. In a way, that's what Laura Ingalls Wilder did metaphorically. I wish my eyes could become pearls that brought dreams in to someone's life. I do my best with my pen."

"What's it to be? Cashmere or beads?"

"My eyes are dazzled still but I'm a grown-up sybarite."

"What of beaded bubbles?"

"I've a weak head—and a weakness for what preys on a weak head."

Nowhere does Jane speak of amethysts—or cat's eyes, or carnelians.

"I probably do passim. I'm not one to overlook a semi-precious stone."

─────

I forgot to be nasty," said Rosewall. "Is it too late to start?"

"You need all your energy for playing in the over-forty-fives," decided Laver. "Pity. If we'd remembered to be nasty, we might have been able to play a bit."

─────

What's so wrong with black knickers, Simon?
Remember Bueno's pink.
Does it alarm you that virginal white
Half-cloaks the colour of ink?

Why not drink
Of her tennis?

─────

Jane has a weakness for sheepskin;
Calista is thought too thin.
Would sheepskin pad out Calista
And help to heal the blister
Of press attention, besides finding a mister?

─────

"I could have sworn that dress was green when I bought it."
   "Shop lights can be deceiving."
   "My hat was green—it always has been, it nearly matches the tiny emerald in my brooch—the one that's so tiny it's hardly worth having a hat to match it—I'll show you..."
   "What's wrong?"
   'The emerald's sort of...colourless...like the dullest jellyfish you've ever seen, or transparent soap. I paid good money for that."
   'There's something odd in the paper. Look at the headline."
   "Which? Oh...blankpeace, blankpeace, continued on page 5, blankpeace.
   That's slipshod printing."
   "Is it? Don't you think it's weird? Look in your wardrobe."
   "Nothing green, nothing greenish. Have I had a selective burglar?"
   "Like the selective printer? And what happened to the emerald? Was it bleached by the sun, lying in a dresser? It's as though green's fighting back after having its name taken in vain."

─────

"Remember what cool-headed Octavian did to Antony, Tony."

─────

A Dream Benefit Match

"We need to be nasty," said Nasser Hussein, "so I've invited Chris Evert and Steffi Graf to teach us how to win."

─────

The Indian army in the second world war was the biggest volunteer army in history, which suggests that Gandhi, who sided with the Japanese, did not have the people in his pocket.

─────

When Claudette Colbert died, I felt sad. I should have summoned television cameras to observe my grief.

─────

Watching cricket under a salman tree,
Thinking of Rushdie under a salman tree,
Watching cricket, forgetting himself
For once, assassination, his second self,
Eluded, puts me in mind of Alamut,
Of the Old Man of the Mountains,
Whose acolytes, drugged and cut
To the quick of their dreams by fountains
In a desert and women in the desert
Of their life, went forth to kill and be
Rewarded.

─────

Angel's "careful" was particularly soft and melodious, emphasising the second syllable; it was reminiscent of the top voice fluttering upwards on the Everly Brothers' "Barbara Allen". They sang "Barb'ry".

─────

Angel had red buttons on her top, worn over lighter red with chevrons. I kept wondering whether her top was one colour, the sleeves becoming shadowed in to burgundy as they hung and a deeper patch of colour being the shadow between her breasts, a Burgundy of vineyards on the slope of the Côte d'Or.

─────

"I dreamed I went back in time and was shipwrecked on Fiji and they ate me. They were nice about it, Ails. They said it was immemorial custom—nothing personal—they would have eaten anyone. The funny thing is, after they'd eaten me, I heard them complimenting the cook. Then I woke up. I don't feel like bacon and eggs after that."

─────

Alf has the look of a man who would like Wilson, Keppel and Betty.

─────

His mother's a Metaxas
But he struggles to pay taxes.
Farms in Scotland, not in Texas,
Are on his scale. Bewail your fate,
Philip, not of Macedon, but of Ithaca,
Bound to your lot, no apothecary's
Draught, no single malt, no nectar
Giving relief from a dead-line.
The dread line: now or sooner
Came before you could cut off your 'phone.
No Jack Russell pupping under your desk
Can afford excuse. Paid hack, alack,
And paid by the yard—never do they lard
Him with praise, never see their way

A Dream Benefit Match

To send him to Florence at the paper's
Expense. His expenses would not keep Bernard Levin
In snacks.

―――――

The planets do not smile on Agnew now, down
To one Mars bar for a match, yearning for the
Familiar latch of home, the familiar clutch
Of offspring, free from worries about
The latest glitch, the latest snatch,
The latest cardboard box of lunch
To munch if he dared. At least, he's there
During Lent. "I'll be a spent force when you see
Me again". Back from the gateway to the Khyber.

―――――

Glenn McGrath is not a waif; Curtley Ambrose is not a waif; the orphans in "Boot Polish" are waifs. (Take note at "The Times").

―――――

"Bradman's on the back foot; that's his fourth four of the over."

―――――

I have better bettered Betjeman
Than you have bettered Betjeman,
Bettered bitter Betjeman as well as lighter Betjeman,
Bullied, guilty Betjeman as well as courting Betjeman,
In thrall to a glowing racquet arm.

―――――

Heliotrope & Hansie

Liz Lochhead locked horns with Mont Sainte Victoire,
Having toiled up its lower slopes. Does she feel stuck
On the lower slopes of poetry? Cézanne found la gloire
Posthumously. Does Liz still hope for such luck?

―――――

"Well, I'll be gormed," said Norm
"And I'll be Normed," said Cliff.
Auden would have added a riff
Of "Sammy, Sammy, Sammy,"
For Carla, that "red-hot mammy"
As she styled herself, preening
Between beers. You'd need more eyes
Than Wackford Squeers to see Norm's
Mental life. "Squeers—that's the Yorkshire Cyclops,"
Cliff would say and live to breathe
Another day.
"You can't gainsay that Squeers had one eye;
So had Polyphemus: ergo, Nicholas Nickleby
Is Odysseus." "Please, Zeus, strike him," implores Carla.
"I resent that. I feel a velleity to do something about it."
Many miseries Norm has drowned.

―――――

The misplaced accent on "Over the hills and far away" niggled me. "Far…" going up and over, to conquer or discover, not "away", sinking back in to naval half-pay, army pensions, wasting their days in brawling in taverns. Whoever arranged it was no romantic and no melodist. The lilt was gone, the exhilaration was gone. What a downbeat England.

―――――

A Dream Benefit Match

Meena liked a swig. In full fig, bejewelled,
She was the frontispiece of a civilisation.
Was she in thought fit emblem of a nation?
Did she drink to live with her beauty, her art,
The weight of expectation? To unwind
You have first to be taut—and she was taut
As millions felt through her, loved and suffered,
Loved to suffer, flew with the swallow,
Limped like a starving ox to a dried-up water-hole,
Revived at the sound of a familiar voice
And felt the emptiness of a voice gone for ever.

─────

Mordecai was a mortified guy
To find himself treated as a spy
When he warned
Against flaming mushrooms in the sky.

─────

'Tampopo', Limpopo,
Parris comes from Limpopo;
Has he ever seen 'Tampopo'?
Surely, he must know Umbopa,
Roped in to find King Solomon's Mines.
Where are the mind's King Solomon's Mines?
Parris would say they're out in the wilds,
Altiplano, not Limpopo.
I'm with Shakespeare, preferring woods
To heath, the blackbird to the hoopoe

─────

Heliotrope & Hansie

Vanunu is a no-no for political campaigners.
Liberal as Pio Nono, they cave in when tested.
Mordecai can rot in gaol, in solitary confinement;
For telling Israel's secrets, these are his days of atonement.
(And what do you say, Greenpeace?
The dreams of fat and lean kine, meant
To teach wisdom and tolerance, fall on deaf ears.)
Will Levin lend his magisterial voice,
Michael Grade his raffish, showman's voice,
Jonathan Miller his know-all director's voice?
Woody Allen would stand up and be counted
If they weren't looking over his head.
'Tis a bed of nails for Vanunu. Worse threatens.
Procrustes is in power in Tel Aviv.

―――――

Rocco blew hot as the Sirocco;
Henshaw's touch was as sure as Crenshaw's;
Paparelli shone like Schiaparelli;
Dobermann was faithful as a dobermann
From the Bernese Oberland, where he might
Have been a Bernese big cheese,
Better than being a Burmese big cheese.
Emmenthal has more holes than Swiss banking.
Duane was everyone's favourite slob
Before taste was such a weather-vane.

―――――

Catching me smiling as she looked across sleepily, my mother smiled contentedly, enjoying the comfortable hour as one who had worked in a factory for nine years, borne children, stood in the playground in childhood with perishing feet—closer to her now than much else—and had learned to see life as a stoical saving up for treats and

A Dream Benefit Match

a resting of the mind in past pleasures. As Gandalf and the elves were able to dream, walking, did she see past hardships before her and know them powerless to hurt her? Did her mind flit back to Ethel M. Dell stories of long ago in which she helped a gentleman with a sprained ankle across a Breton beach and she alone of all the girls in the matchworks was privileged to be his friend?

―――――

Tony Blair's no Harold Lever
Any more than Chester's Deva
Or Glenda Jackson a great diva
Or Mandelson more deft than the weaver
Bird. Blair is the great deceiver.

―――――

Angel's hair crawled out of the 'plane, looking like Dougal from "Magic Roundabout", then her face proved that she was Angel.

―――――

Kamlesh was fretting to talk about cricket but was lumbered with a school inspector who waffled. An hour later, I could remember little that he had said.

"Are you interested in sport?" asked Kamlesh, not very hopefully. Only motor-racing.

'Talking about cricket...' He could contain himself no longer.

―――――

"He's wordy, Wordsworth."
What's a word worth to 'The Times'
From Wordsworth, whether blank or rhymes,
From Larkin, blanker still—a dime's

The rate for Larkin's parkin cake,
Not luscious Black Forest Gateau.

Gozo: I'm waiting for Beckett.
Malta: Beckett? Is he under siege too or has he broken through the enveloping clouds?
Gozo: He's going grape-picking, somewhere near Henry of Navarre country—Henri, the "vert galant". I gave up wearing the green when they laughed at me in Dublin. Malta: You're Beckett—waiting for Beckett.
Gozo: I've been waiting these many years. Sometimes, in a rugby scrum, I used to wonder: "Is that Samuel really me? Will he hear a voice calling, and what will that calling be? Then someone would tread on me and I'd roll aside pronto, the hurly-burly would take over again and I'd be one more muddied oaf waiting for the world to be elucidated.
Malta: Eli was there when Samuel was called.
Gozo: He wasn't there when I wasn't called.
Malta: (pause) Did Paris elucidate?
Gozo: Lights of the Folies Bergères—I moved to another quarter to get away from theatrical people—bit hard when you write plays—lights of shops—light shining through James Joyce's wine glasses, James Joyce's conversation.
Malta: Was he all lit up?
Gozo: Like the fleet. The floating fleet, not the prison. I thought, if I picked grapes, Id hold the key to James Joyce's wits in my hand.
Malta: He's not a beer man then?
Gozo: Dear man? I always got on well with him, except when he was in his cups, which was more often than he was out of them.
Malta: I meant he wasn't one for the beer, the Guinness?
Gozo: In truth, he was a promiscuous drinker. If Lapsang Souchong had made him drunk, he would have drunk it. He

thought it unfair that there wasn't time to sample every alcoholic drink in the world—or pun on every word in the English language. He confided to me that he thought Jesuits had got at God, nobbled him.
Malta: That's a fierce thought: God no kinder than a Jesuit.
Gozo: It's a sock on the nose. When I was treading grapes, I wondered what I was doing being so morose in the sunshine.
Malta: There's a power of cheerfulness in the world.
Gozo: Exactly. I provide some ballast. I'm a Lenten sort of writer. If they want to be uplifted, let them listen to Bach. They can tell me to go to Hell.
Malta: Would you?
Gozo: I'm here.

Chapter Three

Hansie And Grendel

Hansie hied him to Hordwah, hard by Ganga's gloomed
Beyond glaucous depths. Doom came not there.
Sachin, such as Such ne'er bowled at,
Came from south of the Raan of Kutch,
Killing bowling like Jack Ketch.
As Ketchel's teeth stuck in Johnson's glove,
So did the ball stay hit. Hot, humid,
Heaving with expectation of the monsoon,
Indian air throbbed. Thrum, went Hansie's head,
Fingers itching for his fine 'phone's promise of treasure
And, in retirement, pleasure, hard-earned pleasure,
Placed at arm's length, on a tempting length.
A voice out of the void, a voice bugged
By Bharat's bureaucratic tentacles,
Ears on suckers, drew Hansie to his doom
As though he had been lured in to a pentacle.
Oh, that he were listening to Brendel,
Not being hugged by Grendel.

—————

Civilisation is not moving behind the bowler's arm.

—————

Heliotrope & Hansie

Kaletsky's no Lavretsky, no dreaming squire Lavretsky,
Yet did he dream in Oxford, aspiring Anatole?
No. Bow Bells rang the changes, the City still his range is.
He never went west for the hell of it
And liked Reaganomics not a whit.

Leaning on the famous lime within
The boundary at Canterbury, Allan
Border muses on tactics, free of the din
And stress of Tests. The peace, like Lallans
To English, adds a quiet, novel colour
To the game while ghosts of long-dead cricketers
Linger in the lime leaves.

There was something odd about Jeff Thomson. He moved his arms and legs as though he were gangling yet he is burly, strength and suppleness together making him as quick as anyone has ever been.

For Simon Barnes, sport and literature are so entwined that he is sick as Flaubert's parrot.

Turgenev is a way in to Russian history as the Volga was a way in to the Russian interior and the Mississippi-Missouri was a way in to the American interior.

Hansie And Grendel

"Listen to the ocean".
Nina and Frederick split up,
As did Thor Heyerdahl and the girl with bushy blonde hair.
Did they listen to the ocean more than to each other?

—————

Towards Ostende
The sea-chop quickens,
Comma-d in short swift waves
Which answer the flickering beacons
On the shore as guitar
To violin.

—————

Browning's crowning glory was not his bucking rhythm,
Rumbustious tales, novelist's imagery, nose for character,
But a blend of all, grappling with all
And undeterred withal by his own aberrations.

—————

Felicity likes Marvell.
I marvel at Felicity,
Being accursed of the stars.
Whole of the stars, Felicity
Seems closer to Andrew Marvell
Than to dullard Stoppard's wit.
Intellectual? And highbrow. Sweet
On the ear and sweet in the senses
Flowing from the mind.
Fruit in Marvell. Fruit on the tongue. Sex in Marvell—
Oh, Felicity, baring her heart 'neath
A mosquito-net of seventeenth century

Heliotrope & Hansie

Subtlety. Andrew's quiddity
Is the full quid for Felicity,
His garden her garden, his soothing
Melody hers, his thorns of wit piquant.

─────

Martin Amis, Martinmas,
Does Martin Amis go to mass?
Martin Luther brought to pass
That Northerners wouldn't go to Mass.
Would Martin Amis let it pass
If lesser lights were warmed at the fire
Of his burnt books?

─────

"Broadcasting is like an offside trap; it won't work if someone fails to move up. Everyone must hate the same people and be sycophantic to the same people. Hate list; toady list. Put them on your lap-top. The most important names should be on a card in your pocket at all times, like German declensions."

─────

"I was walking in this wise," said Eric Morecambe, "which means I had a fat hairy wig on my legs, but I couldn't make them little. "Eric: or little by little"—it's the story of my decline, ruined by drink and bad company—or drink in good company, it's all the same, give or take a few pints, jokes, pint-sized jokers. Take a card, I mean a card in Arnold Bennet's case—a hard case, who was played by a smart Alec—bringing us round from drink to Guinness and Eric to Alec, so the Bedser twins have the last word. It's not easy finding a wig for legs. Women are very keen on waxing but, when it comes to waning, they're waiting for their demon lover. That is another side of Ernie

Hansie And Grendel

Wise: demon lover, quicker than the demon bowler and swerving from one bed-post to another. He used to send valentines to "another lady what I have loved", and they loved him back, to distraction. Strange as it may seem, Erroll Flynn could not hold a candle to him—or near him, without singeing his hairy legs. I've known people sing his legs too, and not joking. They would have launched a thousand ships. Betty Grable, remember Betty Grable, was not more sought after—he would keep stealing hub-caps. His head was the only part of him that could keep in step with his legs, being equally admired but a mite more cerebral. Women saw him as a mite— might or might not. He saw himself as a swashbuckler manqué. I let him be Gene Kelly, so far as he could be, and that kept him on his toes. You can't slack if you're trying to be Gene Kelly."

―――――

"We Punjabi fly-by-nighties have our knives and forks in to Blighty's media, which we make steamier while rejecting the myth of the sensual East, which we knock on the head like a king cobra in a king bed in the master bedroom, renamed the maharani's bedroom."

―――――

He's no rugby player, like Rives,
Nor a burly prop from Brive.
He's no empire-builder, like Clive;
Nor greatly sought-after to wive;
He's no master-novelist, like James,
Nor a wicket-keeper like Ames.
He's the build of some pantomime dames
Yet he's partial to the tango
Is Clive James.

―――――

Heliotrope & Hansie

Hogwood has not the charm of the dogwood
In Morrison's eyes or, rather, Morrison's ears.
He likes some zing in his antique music.
Purcell, like Mozart, can be both childlike and moving,
Says Morrison. Does he wish that he could?

─────

No condom, no condo.
No condom, trust Condee.
Take your ease with a breeze that is sweetness,
Forsaking pianos to help us bring completeness.
No condom, trust Condee.
Clinton's promises were just tooth-rotting candy.
He would not jump ship, so we'll sing him ashore with a shanty.
He fought slavery like the king of the Ashanti
Or a home-loving boy from the wastes of Dahomey,
With a regiment of women who meant men harm and America
   no good.
But he thought he had the wood on his opponents.
So devout was he that he went forth to multiply,
Making new voters from his own seed.
And he never inhaled the weed.
No condom, trust Condee.
No condom, no condo.
Where? Oh, where? Oh, where
Is my condo?
Please find me one pronto.
(inspired by Bob Marley and Condoleezza Rice before she was tested by office.)

─────

What do you see in e-mail?
The rings of Saturn? Jupiter risen?

Hansie And Grendel

Bob Marley singing release from prison?
Is Marley Jamaica's prism?
Is Marley Jamaica's what might have been?
Marley was dead at the start of the tale.
Was Marley's death but the start of the tale
As his songs make rings in the Caribbean?
Port Royal went under the sea not far from where Marley lived.

―――――

Yuri sought to urinate;
A shot in the Arctic;
Straggler. Blood flowed.

―――――

Big, black bogeymen
Taken to the heart of the Oval;
Happiness.

―――――

Tony Blair is like an American television evangelist. Inclined to hysteria, he whips up hysteria in others.

―――――

Twin towers tongue, forever falling, forever blazing, tongue of fire, tongue of fashionable shoes that follow in the footsteps of Dunblane, Diana.
    Twin towers tongue, in unison, ad nauseam—Nuremberg never saw such regimented drumming, drumming up support for killing. Will the populace be willing?
    Twin towers tongue—there's a place in hell for those who dwell on falling towers for lack of an easier way to fill a purse.

Get a mind, get out more, look at the world, not the monitor.
Twin towers tongue, heard of Dresden, Hamburg, Tokyo?
Current affairs broadcasters watch their favourite fawlty towers falling forever.

—————

The world changed, David E. Kelly, when Americans started supporting Fenian murderers a century and a half ago.

—————

The Pawnees are on their knees;
The Sioux will have to sue
For peace; the Comanche
Will hear reveille
When conscripted. They'll rue
The day when Uncle Sam
Came their way, cruel
And crooked as Uncle Joe
Stalin. Alistair Cooke boasts
Of mass production of ships
And thinks the greatest lord of hosts
Is in the White House, but Kipling
Knew a greater lord of hosts.
God is in the still, small voice,
Not the Yankee bellow.

—————

Oh, what avail if Anna Friel
Should take the veil before you feel
Her charms? Why then you'd rail
Against the custom of taking the veil.

—————

Hansie And Grendel

"Great Britain has carried out a surgical strike on the I. R. A. bases of New York, Boston and Hollywood. Unfortunately, San Francisco was collateralled."

―――――

Will Helena play Hermia
And Hermia play Helena
And Justine maybe Lamia
In a setting infinitely balmier
Than England? One wins the palm, Another needs the balm
Of friends' applause.

―――――

Which is the squirmier, Helena or Hermia,
When you hold them off Terra Firma,
Probing Terra Incognita, as Donne would say,
When so much was incognita, or Hughes
In a time of cognition, Hughes with his cheek,
Great cleft of cheek,
Riven, rivulet of blood foretelling his fate?
His late wife is his fate. His late wife baits
Him. Ingrate, he is called by those who use her,
Who appropriate her grief.

―――――

A variant on "Lost Horizon: Cool Tony is taken to a valley where coolness can be retained for centuries but, if he steps outside, his coolness will evaporate and he will become an ordinary warm human being.

―――――

"Wallies of the world, unite. You have nothing to lose but your scorn." read the banner at the head of the multitude led by William Hague through central London, bearing lifesize pictures of Wally Hammond, Wally Barnes and Wally Grout. In memory of Wally Ralegh, they spread a mackintosh over one of the deepest of the potholes left by a Labour council in a Conservative ward. An I. T. N. woman, sent to interview them, stepped on it and sank to her thighs. Being chivalrous, they helped her out and besought a cup of tea from Allen Coren, who had come to watch, equipped with Test Match flask.

"Say when," he told the chattering-teethed broadcaster. The wallies took the opportunity to ask the question that is on all lips:

"What were you thinking of when you perpetrated Giles?"

"My next smoke, most likely—it was before antirrhinums. Antediluvian, almost. I too am a wally," he declared. "I've been a wally, man and boy, these many years." So he went along with them.

'This jogs my memory, vaguely, of the German footballer, Fritz Walter long ago.'

Coren took a sip of brandy to his memory, then suddenly saw the headline: "I. T. N. girl inebriated; Coren implicated," and would have blanched but he was beyond blanching.

"Do you think that Wallace Beery would have been the mayor for London?' he asked, but Hague was not with him.

"Picture his Long John Silver," elucidated Coren. "He would have raised the tone of metropolitan politics—and added some colour. He would have put the fear of God in to council taxpayers and council employees who got above themselves. Just the ticket."

Hague led them to the B. B. C. Television Centre, where they had a minute's silence in memory of public broadcasting. Cowed by walliedom rampant, the plutocrat populists of Channel 4 promised to mend their ways, turning their back on Bazalgette, unworthy descendant of the great Bazalgette, and his like.

'To Wapping" was now Hague's battle-cry. The wally with a first from Oxford led them to the portals of 'The Times", past young women with debased degrees, and Peter Stothard found himself

Hansie And Grendel

"middle in the throng", as Virgil says. Hague challenged him to the best of three throws and duly bested him (pinstripe pinned, though he has many dressing down days).

"It's all Major's fault, you know," said Stothard, "siding with the established British television companies against Rupert Murdoch. We had no choice—well, we need not have employed certain people..."

"I can take knocks," interrupted Hague. "I'm not one for the bleeding heart. I'm not a Tony-winning Tony. But some people are sensitive about your abuse." He brandished a sheaf of letters of support from foreign entertainers and sportsmen. Stothard made a mental note to retire soon and let someone else be responsible for Caitlin Moran. As an olive branch, he gave Hague the poems of Walther von der Vogelweide, honorary wally, to make him a rounded William.

"If you don't like it, pass it on to me," said Coren. "Not many laughs, but he's good."

Editor and wally shook hands and Hague withdrew, mollified, with his legions—for now.

Japonica, japonica,
You should buy one, Monica,
Better far than brassica,
Not as odorous as arabica,
But quince—ah, quince,
A jelly pure as Peter Quince
To bring the magical in to life
When you are skint
And people around you more like Peter Quint.
You careful planner but scrumptious bint,
Your future lies, sweet Monica,
With japonica.

"Darrell Hair is fond of shirts that shade of blue," said Peter Roebuck, "and he likes grilled sole with a slice of lemon and a smidgeon of tarragon. That Chardonnay's not Darrell Hair's Chardonnay. I know precisely the sort that pleases his palate. I know the tune he hums when he goes out to the wicket on a wet day. I'm a veritable clever clogs where Darrell Hair is concerned. "What's my motivation?" Ask Roebuck. It would have saved Marlon Brando trouble if he had had Roebuck to tell him about his motivation. Darrell Hair's mind is a seething Rotorua of racial resentment and prejudice. He doesn't think so but I know better. I can outBrearley Brearley. He doesn't see Shoaib Akhtar straining every sinew to bowl a hundred mile per hour ball; he sees a bowler neglecting to hone his skills. What if he does? If Shoaib Akhtar aims at becoming a media star, not a great bowler, that's up to him. What is great anyway? I was at Cambridge when greatness had been thrown out the window—and there are no great lawyers now, except Hailsham and Ally McBeal: he's a classicist and she's skinny, so the media are obsessed with her bones. Make no bones about it, we're all dispensable, even Vivian Richards and Joel Garner."

(Written in 2002 or '03. Roebuck said Aborigines are only kept out of the Australian cricket team by racism. Indians outnumber Aborigines by two thousand to one. Not many Indians would have got in to the Australian Test team since 1989, fewer Englishmen.)

─────

Turgenev was reminded of Russia by the smell of hemp. Which are the most evocative scents in India? Does the Gita prescribe aromas as an aid to meditation?

─────

How can a country be civilised which colourises classic films?

─────

Hansie And Grendel

Did Trilby like astilbe, pink on her cheeks, astilbe?
When she poses for Svengali, deceiver bound not for Bali,
She shows more than a charlie, as Barry Norman would say,
And gay is the sight of her charms as pink as astilbe.

―――――

'The score is 586 for 2 but the body language is magnificent. Just watch those slips strut."

―――――

"Rosewall's looking weary."
 "He always looks like that."
 Rosewall was one of the best tennis players in the world from eighteen to thirty-nine, longer than anyone else.

Chapter Four

Canterbury Bells

"I need counselling," grumbled Captain Bligh. "I've been humiliated and bereft of my ship. You needn't expect me to navigate you four thousand miles to safety."

―――――

Vilas from the Pampas,
Metronomic as Sampras,
According to the B. B. C.,
Found Paris shale suited him to a -t.
More sand than clay, it looked to me.
Nastase plays in my rêverie.

―――――

Hail to Hayley, hail to Kirsty,
Lither than Hebridean silkie;
Hayley's downcast, Noah's thirsty,
Riding drunkenly, but Kirsty
Never stumbles; Alf never bumbles;
Brodie hugs lava to her heart
Like a nymph on Mount Etna. Faun,
Alex, faun. Dani, more decorous than Danae,
Sees Sally's face in her green eye.
Fletcher shooting Cupid's arrows?

Fletcher, blameless tutor? Who's kidding?
"I'll do no-one's bidding," says Noah.

—————

Brodie's hair is bouclé, like Claudette Colbert's. Why is Noah's hair outlandishly streaked? Brown over blonde. You'd think he had been mown in patterns like a cricket square—rather, the streaks curl like Medusa's snakes. Not very natural, Noah.

—————

Brodie moves like a thirteen-year-old at seventeen: that is part of the character.

—————

"I decided over breakfast," said Tony Blair, 'to realign Mars. It ought to be nearer the Earth. It's the People's planet and the People have a right to see it clearly. So I've set up a committee of my scientists who will report soon and I shall proceed with all expedition to drag Mars in to the twenty-first century. Michael Howard was Home Secretary in a government which did nothing about bringing Mars within sight of the People. Furthermore, we are confidently working on a plan to provide holidays on Mars for deserving citizens. Never let it be said that Mars bars the way to Labour."

—————

I'm not to be suborned;
I'm not to be shoe-horned
In to a pressure group

—————

Canterbury Bells

"Your coolness is metaphysical: it is beyond ice and snow; it is the wonder of every fakir. But coolness is a fragile thing, Tony. You could slough it off unawares and you would not be chuffed if that happened."

―――――

Americans have planted their flag on Dani's chest. What do they think she is? Iwojima?

―――――

"Green and saffron are both colours in the Indian flag. Neither should try to take over the whole flag." Ironically, the colours are given in English, the unifying language from faraway.

―――――

Words, Wordsworth, nothing but words.
Paint London. Let London live if such be your intent
And if your bent is for scene-painting. How could you
Of the hills love London?
Stepping out in my London,
Not for me the Steppes and forests,
Not for me the lakes and fells;
London sounds the death-knell
Of my poetry. I can't kick my heels up any more.
I can't shout my feeling for the crags, healing me by their echo.
Rustic William has become a Metropolitan of letters, laureate no less, uttering platitudes to please the London palate, not the ear, for where's the music now? Where is the furrowed brow of creation? I scorned the books. Now I scorn the country feeling.

―――――

Porteous is the man for me,
From a practice in the old country
Of a new country, Porteous
Is the man for me, righteous
Porteous, slickest scalpel, bounteous
Host, for the ladies far and wide a toast.
He's a lord of the vine in his spare time.
It makes him much more than a dime.
Loneliness is a lime for a country doctor.

─────

"I did not betray Britain to a foreign power at noon on August 10th," said Alastair Campbell, (aside) "it was just after three on August 19th."
    "An independent judge will conduct an inquiry," said Tony Blair. "His remit will be to establish whether there is any substance in allegations relating to Alastair Campbell's conduct at noon on August 10th. Events on any other day are beyond the scope of the inquiry."

─────

"I haven't sold out to Hollywood."
    "You sold out to Murdoch."
    "He let me make my film."
    "He let you make his film."
    "Gallipoli is mine—all mine—not a jot of Murdoch, not a shot of Murdoch, not a product placement detail. You could say there's more of John Ford in the landscapes, the sweep of the Western Australian desert, Egypt—not so much Egypt."

─────

"Enough of your grape gripes, Niles. My offering is very acceptable to those who don't shun the byways of oenology. Time was when your mind was more open to such serendipities."

Canterbury Bells

"If that's serendipity, I'm Nefertiti. Classic, Frasier. We must swear by the classic if we are to judge the exotic. That has more kick than flavour. I don't want to drink a mule. And I'll give koumiss a miss."
"Koumiss! You wound me, Niles."
(In the spirit of a Bach variation)

─────

"Where's my serpent of old Niles?" "She's seeing a patient."

─────

"We can have too much of the common man," declared Frasier.

─────

'The Niles for President bandwagon is gathering force."

─────

Frasier and Niles are amiable snobs. In the later series, some writers seemed to dislike them.

─────

Put the mockers on the Ockers on the Sydney Bridge,
Then we'll surely level the score.
They haven't such fine legs as Cyd Charisse
But, when they play, there are bloomers galore.
Aussies in their cossies are as white as whey
'Cos they have to wear a barrier cream.
Betting-mad, they've seen more of Mill Reef
Than the Barrier Reef.

─────

Surely, D. N. A. does not come in all the colours which show up on a computer. "If so, we have the creator's colour sense. Which painter comes nearest to it?"

─────

Kate Muir likes vulgarity,
Not Parisian solemnity.
Intellectuals, up to their hocks in the trough,
Make much of metal genitalia, inter alia.
A hex on such intellectual sex.
Provincials come for Courbet; likewise Kate.
She keeps a look-out for something good in skips
But consigns to skips pseudo-philosophy.
Kate fancies herself as a scourge of intellectuals,
Glaswegian gimlet boring holes in their waffle.
(She tiptoes around the concierge.)
She grew out of Plath, did not need
To grow out of de Beauvoir.
She likes her sex with humour, thus humanised.

─────

What joy to see Coach again. He and Diane gave the first two series of "Cheers" a warmth which it only had spasmodically in later years. Sam is fond of Coach, who is fond of Diane. Sam feels protective towards them both, which brings out the best in him. By the fourth series, Diane is more affected, more of a snob, and Sam is more stupid. (He had been intelligent enough to read "War and Peace" in a few days.) The contrast between Diane and the others, particularly Carla, is more satisfying than the setting down of intellectual Frasier in the bar. Frasier chimes with Niles.

─────

Canterbury Bells

Snooty Shruti turned me down.
I'm the coolest man-about-town.
Shruti's silly.
I'm the handsomest man in Dilhi.
Shruti's hot as southern chilli
But she's silly
Shruti.

─────

Is the melody of the Gita part of its meaning? Are there sacred sequences of vowels and consonants? Did people once find more illumination in illumination than in the text?
"The Holy Book must glow through the reader's every word and deed, as piddocks shone through the lips and hands of the eater."

─────

Will Poppy and Emma sing me to sleep?
Will opiate of Weelkes bring me hours of slumber?
I'm just a back number of poetry,
Known only north of the Humber
And there an outsider, an outlier of southern culture;
In the south, a northerner.
(early, before I was known south of the Humber.)

─────

"I'm a loner, not a loser,
I'd be at home in the palace at Susa,
I'd have given Alexander a bloody nose.
I'm the nemesis of Blair,
Jumped up lawyer without flair.
I could sweep the floors of Westminster with his hair.

─────

Heliotrope & Hansie

Mahadji's sweets reminded me of those Miss Condliffe laid on each desk before afternoon school when we had given her an end-of-year present. Another year she gave us each a small bar of chocolate.

The way to stop the phalanx was to starve it, pick off men from a distance, take it in the rear...and rear...and rear, ever changing the angle of attack. Napoleon or Genghis Khan would have made short work of Alexander the drunkard.

Had they foibles, Brueghels, elder, younger and the rest of the tribe? Did they imbibe schnapps to excess? Did they leave their business in the lap of the gods? Were they at odds with each other and their time or did they sit cosily near the apex of bourgeois life in Holland, the coming nation? Did they have their ration of sins?

I don't beat about the bush, I should rather beat up Bush
Before I admire the glories of Isfahan.
Desperate Dan had hairs to pull.
You'd think he lived on the Isle of Mull,
For he never shaved from one year's end to another.
It was Dundee made him tough, cow's pie, never Dundee cake,
So he lived and played so rough
He would have belonged in Service's "Songs of a Sourdough".
But some say Dan has a glass jaw
When he crosses the Atlantic.
Those on "grass" make crass law
Across the Atlantic.

Canterbury Bells

"What a mazy dribble by Tessa Jowell. Jack Lang won the World Cup for France in 1998. Can she do the same? It's reassuring to have a minister of culture who can pass, even if it's only the buck."

According to the B. B. C., French football was boring from 1958 to '81 because there was a conservative government. When socialists were elected in 1981, Platini became exciting overnight. The period from 1958 to '81 was very rich for French films and popular songs.

―――――

"Walter von der Vögelweide's Palestine Song has made an incursion in to the first movement of Shostakovich's "Leningrad" symphony— a rousing drive—now it has bit in to the bolero, the Leningrad Symphony is in disarray—more than usual—the Palestine Song has kicked its backside, driven it from the field and thrown its megaphone after it." (written after being trapped washing dishes during a relentless ostinato in the fourth symphony.)

―――――

Canterbury bells for Canterbury belles—
Did Copperfield hand them to their coach,
Their faces framed by white and lilac flowers on tall stems,
Their every whim a blessing for a young man fresh from the wen?
Long afterwards, the name, Canterbury,
Reverberated in his memory, where time can bury
But not erase. Bells he could hear he hated;
These he loved.

(Dickens found church bells cacophonous. Copperfield is the character nearest to being his alter ego.)

―――――

I'd never grass on Gunther Grass,
Though his conscience be not clear as glass.
It would have come to a pretty pass
If I should grass on Gunther Grass.
Now Fischer's a fish of a different water,
Clotting German polity's aorta.

―――――

O'Connor: Pavarotti may be able to sing but what use is he as a stagehand? Has he taken a course in the theory and practice of operatic production? Has he a diploma saying he can reach out to the masses, make opera relevant, relating it to the environment of the underprivileged? The modern "La Bohème" is for underachievers, the disabled, single parents—it must be a team effort. Pavarotti can't be a prima donna; we have Cherie Blair. What he needs is ten years' re-education, working in a factory.

―――――

Why is Beethoven thought to reconcile more than Bach? "Beethoven reconciles man with man, Bach Man with God." An easy distinction. Is it true?

―――――

As Alex mocked Brodie, he praised her.

―――――

Alex's scything tackle nearly took Jade's legs away. Danny Raco's Italian blood will out. Patrick Vieira would have tackled her like a gentleman.

―――――

Canterbury Bells

Without Zidane, it was Sedan. (the 2002 World Cup).

———

I'll answer the daffodils in rills of running sound worthy of Ezra Pound. Yet not for daffodils amid the hills do I sing but for the blue of Asia Minor. Helen must have looked on grape hyacinths and doubtless decked herself with them. Whence came the grapes in their name, for they are not bacchic flowers?

———

The poems of Hafiz sound erotic to me.
There is not much rising above sensuality.
Oh, what a wheeze to translate Hafiz
And put your own name to it.
You'd get the kudos instead of being
An anonymous conduit.

———

Are there Sufi poems any more spiritual and mystical than the poems of Mallarmé?

———

Who is Sylvia? Who is Ted?
Just two poets, long since dead.
They say that Ted first led;
Acclaimed, she weighed him down like lead,
His reputation plunging to elevate hers.

———

Less of a leper than Leporello,
He's still distrusted is Portillo.
Fear of foreigners bred Martello
Towers; besides, he's smooth as brillo
Pads are rough, and it's a suspect
Smoothness as the loi des suspects
Could pop out of the bottle.
Some would say that, on his mettle,
Michael Portillo has no bottle,
Smooth as a silk but not Kilroy-Silk,
Crooked as a silk but not Kilroy-Silk.

─────

One more for the Gipper
As cheers ring out to the Big Dipper
For the man who thought the stars
And stripes were limitless
And heaven could be reflected on earth
In simple pleasures.

─────

Shirley Williams' nastiness about Reagan is coupled with a pretence that any leader of the Liberal Democrats is saintly.

─────

Whichever 'Times" idiot wrote the obituary of Reagan will go down in history as having written "at the height of the Depression". In the depths of the Depression. You can't say "up a coal-mine". I read the 'Times" report of Disraeli's death in my first weeks at university. You're nailed for posterity.

─────

Canterbury Bells

It's axiomatic that Ixiolirion
Is prettier far than the Silmarillion.
Purple in spring is Ixiolirion,
Tyrian to pick from a motor-bike pillion,
Tyrian within reach of the poorest scullion,
Who can feel as rich as if he had bullion
And not an eked-out Silmarillion,
Posthumous fare to sell a million,
Not as straight as Imogen's Posthumus,
Nor a patch on an Ixiolirion.

—————

You win some, you lose some
And yet you're always winsome.
At times you feel like flotsam
Or even Nick Smith's jetsam.
Dancing, you are lissom;
Your smile can soothe like balsam.
Sensible now, you've done some
Silly things but risen above them.
Your eyes could ransom
Half the world
And leave the rest yearning.

—————

Eloise is a breeze on Max's cheeks;
For Eloise he knows his "p"s and "q"s,
Eloise holds the keys to Max's heart,
Which Max himself had never seen.
This knight holds his fees of Eloise.
He'd have stood by her in the time of the Guises
When blood ran red in the streets,
For his strength would have nursed the red in her cheeks

And made her, short-lived, happy.
Max would not have been left with the lees
Of a draught, however much he mourned.
He would have grasped her knees as Odysseus those of Nausicaa,
Feeling as though he had crossed uncharted seas,
Ready to laugh at any wheeze, even to the last.

―――――

Reagan had more acumen than a gun-toting Wyatt Earp
And yet he was thought a twerp.
He had horse sense a-plenty, a nose for stocks and shares
And he timed the changeover from swords to ploughshares
To keep freedom's flag flying and undermine the Berlin Wall
And yet this is not to his credit at all,
Say his critics of the left. His playing of the populace
Was deft, yet he never considered himself cool.
He staved off Armageddon. Those who talked of Armageddon
Continued to carp in their ornamental pools.

―――――

The Spirit of De Wet
De Menezes came from Brazil,
Not knowing he was something to kill
Like lighting a fag with a spill
Or riding a bicycle downhill
To the Met.
Jean Charles is a French name.
"We eat Frogs for breakfast," say the Met.
They don't like Germans either.
"We burn Krauts like toast," say the Met.
They starved Boer children
But they never caught De Wet
And, wherever the Met

Canterbury Bells

Threatens, it is countered by
The spirit of De Wet.

—————

They killed Blair Peach, and others too.
Now we have two Blairs to impeach.

—————

It's the Krays that stick in the craw;
Hobnobbing outside the law.

—————

"Alex Ferguson has given me a racehorse," said Tony Blair. "I'm going to make it a life peer."

—————

"We should sail up the Medway," said Da Gama, "like the Dutch. It's traditional."
"With your name, you would say that," retorted Edson Carlos Reizenberg. "We must slip up the Thames under cover of our latest technology. The English author, Douglas Duff—better than Ian Fleming—thought of stealth warships long before stealth bombers. Our scientists were intrigued and have long been working to perfect Brazil's secret weapon. Our ships will arrive within range of Metropolitan Police headquarters, then materialise. Our prime target is, of course, blow-your-face-to-hell Stevens. A snatch party will go ashore—hardened men, who can stand the noxious atmosphere of London—and, if fortune favours us, he will be hanged from the yard-arm as a Neapolitan admiral was hanged by Nelson."
"Should we not strike at Parliament?" asked Da Gama. "And at Buckingham Palace?"

'The royal family have been elbowed aside by Blair; they merely fill gossip columns and keep Sky News employed. A broadside against the Commons is a good idea." Reizenberg paused, considering how long the operation would take.

"We could, of course, blow London off the face of the Earth but that would be very American, not civilised."

─────

Was Cantinflas mere candyfloss
While Fàbregas was born to boss
A football field artistically?
(early 2005)

─────

It's pertinent that Gilberto Silva
Blocked while Henry wriggled like an elver
And, when Silva was absent, Arsenal
Turned to bronze, lacking the colour
Of Venice's arsenal or Venice's anything.
Fire, not cannonballs, but fireworks,
Gunners. Gandalf the sky. Come Chelsea,
Cap a pié, you'll put them to flight
More stylishly than Ian Wright.

─────

Begin the beguine with "Naguine";
Negate the beguine with "Naguine"
And all in a marine
Setting, with no city fretting, aquamarine
The colour and mood. By the rood,
This would lift the spirits of Edwin Drood.

─────

Canterbury Bells

Why on earth does Boonya carry a bag of hot coals below her belly? How does she get them the right temperature? Rushdie's characters don't spring to life: his clown can't compare with Raj Kapoor's clown. Can he explain terrorism as well as Fiza? Has Rushdie green or blue eyes? If not, does that mean he is an inferior sort of Kashmiri, not the full Kashmiri? If descended from Macedonian soldiers, Rushdie would be a Greek horse, left outside Cambridge University, then the Indian subcontinent. What about Rugby? He was surely subversive there. He would have been ashamed not to be subversive.

"I was a footnote in the Footlights."

"I was a grace note in Leeds history department."

According to Duncan Ferguson, Warne and McGrath can spend seven and a half minutes off the field and ten minutes on continuously throughout a five Test series. That will prolong their careers. Pakistanis will gather from all over the world for Inzamam-ul-Haq, delighted at being vicariously fleet of foot, to select his twenty substitutes for the series.

"What was that flash?"

"Inzamam—or his substitute."

"We can't play. It's too wet/dusty/muddy/murky. We don't like the taste of the ball when we lick it. Playing regulations stipulated a peppermint flavour." Is Michael Vaughan a throwback to Brearley, who insisted on picking the Pakistan team, having previously joined the campaign to force D'Oliviera on the M. C. C. selectors?

Heliotrope & Hansie

In Pakistani Kashmir, men carried their daughters or sister over the mountains to seek medical help. Yet this is the region where women are deemed worthless, according to Burchill.

―――――

If Joyce had written dimmed fit to play, it would have been hailed as a stroke of genius.

―――――

Oh, what could mar my Waldemar,
Born under such an auspicious star?
He's vaulting is my Waldemar,
Far higher than the Earl of Mar.
He quips at Leonardo's shortcomings
And would, no doubt, have the measure of e. e. cummings.
Upper case, lower case, hard case like Caravaggio,
They're all the same to one who has seen Robert Baggio
But would rather lead the people to art.
When first—and last—did Waldemar feel Cupid's dart
And was he as dizzy as before jewels in Topkapi?
'Top loving; Topkapi,' he might say to his beloved,
Turning her in to an orchard of jewels that might make Baudelaire
Bat an eyelid. Is his artist's lair well away from the editor?

Chapter Five

Bluer Than Oxalis

BLUER THAN OXALIS
Oxalis gives no digitalis
And yet it quickens the heart.
Novalis fell in love with blue,
Bluer than oxalis, filling his heart
With internal skies he came to prize
More than worldly happiness. His blue
Stabbed, yet was a ladder to heaven,
Floral sunbeam, blue sunbeam, lifting
Via lofty thoughts, alchemised
From a flower. Oxalis
Was not quite the flower of Novalis
Yet quickens the heart like digitalis.

―――――

Mickelson holed a muckle putts,
Deadly as a sharpshooter in the butts.
Couples to the green ran smooth
But needed salvation from General Booth
When putt after putt lipped the hole.
Ruefully, he smiled but he smiled.
Who could be downcast at Augusta?

―――――

Heliotrope & Hansie

"My range is from Seamus to Titmus," said C. M. J.,
"I can turn on a sixpence, rhyme on a buss and a cuss
Or even Russ Conway, ephemeral ivory-tinkler,
Or the German show-jumper, Herr Winkler,
Or an English batsman, thought a wuss,
Or even digress with my thoughts on L. B. J.."

―――――

"I may only have a bicycle," said Boris, "but I ride to the sound of cannons."

―――――

"Playing Rosewall, I see," said Gamble as my mother and I crossed the bridge to the park, carrying tennis racquets. My mother thought it unsporting not to play the ball back to her opponent. On the other hand, she told me I had to stand behind the baseline when receiving her service. It kept bouncing twice before I could reach it.

―――――

I can imagine Jacques Brel singing Figaro's first aria or writing it.

―――――

Even when I've had a rheum, I've said: whom.
Travellers on the way to Rum or tracking down Rumi
Have said: whom. When there was no room
At the inn, they said: whom. Debasement
Of the language may loom but we'll still
Say: whom.
(on reading that whom is "semi-obsolete")

―――――

Bluer Than Oxalis

The blue water-lily was sacred to Ancient Egyptians. Napoleon's expedition of 1798-9 rediscovered Ancient Egypt for modern Egyptians as well as for Europeans. Blue water-lilies were studied by French botanists (including some from tombs) and everything learned about Egypt past and present was published in ten folio volumes. Novalis presumably died too early to have seen illustrations, certainly before hieroglyphs were deciphered, so he was writing about his blue flower, a symbol of romantic longing, just as the blue water-lily entered European consciousness but before its significance had been understood.

―――――

"When I'm planning my summer holiday," said Roy, "my trumpet-playing is ornate, to get me in the mood for sunshine and sensuality. This is lifter's ornament, sinewy, the way Fats Waller would have played if he had been Thins."

―――――

"I like Brubeck because he's an explorer," said Roy.

―――――

John Wayne was never a weather-vane;
He stood four-square, bluff John.
He was a jewel but never a Blue John,
Rather a spokesman for fly-over red,
Blue-collar workers, who feared to be freed
By Ring Lardner Junior, fresh from Stalin.
Is it true that Stalin wanted Wayne dead?
What a compliment. He saw show trials,
Did Ring, yet still believed. Nothing
Rang in Ring's head, no freedom bell.
John Wayne was the bane of liberals,

In the American sense, not nineteenth century
Liberals, who respected individuals.

―――――

"Now you're standing for union president," said Peter, "you'd better stop rushing round corners in to girls."

―――――

Agapanthus, Agamemnon:
Moved like a panther, Agamemnon;
Not with an eye for beauty. Blue
Agapanthus soothes the soul
At the other end of light from red.
He died in his bath, not his bed,
Did Agamemnon, warrior head.

―――――

Does Philip prefer agapanthus to Agamemnon, phlox to the flux of time? Is every man a Caesar in his garden?

―――――

"It's in my contract," said Ashley Cole. "I'm entitled to three hours banter a week, best London banter—I don't think Theo Walcott's up to it—raised in Berkshire, played for Southampton. Jens Lehman's doing his best but he doesn't quite hit the funnybone—now that's something the lads laugh at."

―――――

"Boot Polish"
No-one can shine like Bhola

Bluer Than Oxalis

Unless they shine like Bhelu
And all is fine when they see their face
In shoes that mean they have a place
In the world; tea and bread are theirs.

―――――

He polished his way to fortune in his mind's eye. He polished shoes with such pride they might have been the Koh-i-Noor.

―――――

It was a cause for lasting regret that I put the French girl's tip in the same pocket as Bill Beresford's money. I could have bought an orange squash and savoured all the way down the glass her having bought it for me.

―――――

"People may be poor but they're not in poverty." My mother found the distinction important. Poor people had self-respect; those in poverty had not.

―――――

"I con," said the art-dealer. "I con from Byzantium to Hollywood."

―――――

Was Chataway a chatterbox
In the days when he had ruddy locks
And chose to run for Oxford
While some lightweight cox
Gave orders to the hearties?
Did those dropping away think Bannister's

Finishing spurt as deadly as cannister?
He found a place on "Panorama",
Chataway. He went thataway,
The Commons. He wasn't quick enough
For them to say that when he ran.

—————

Mickey Stewart was an improvement on the bad old days of May, Dexter and Illingworth. David Lloyd was an improvement on the bad old days of Mickey Stewart. Duncan Ferguson was an improvement on the bad old days of David Lloyd.

—————

Is Federer the sunset of tennis?

—————

Is Prescott the best you can do, Tony?
The Prescott who wrote of Peru, Tony,
Was articulate, had a grasp of history,
Not a grasp of his secretary. You could
Have left him in charge. You can't leave John at large
Safely. And why fly at the cost of global warming?
Try going by Shanks's pony, Tony. Do your bit
Before Hague returns from his life of Pitt
And invokes the Hague convention against your allies.

—————

"Do young people long for innocence, now that depravity is taken for granted?"

—————

Bluer Than Oxalis

Makelele would never wield a shillelagh,
Sissoko hit you on the boko—
I should Coco, say the knowing.
Merciless as Sid Going,
Some of these ball-winners are.
Diving is frowned on, stamping not.
To the media Wayne Rooney is not
To be judged like lesser mortals,
Less bankable mortals. Xerxes' Immortals
Met their match before the one he predicted, mortality.

—————

My father disliked the way Brazilians sought to humiliate their opponents by showing off in the dying minutes when they had the game won—much as Muhammed Ali taunted opponents and kept them on their feet to inflict more punishment instead of knocking them out.

—————

Lalitha comforted her uncle by stroking elbow, shoulder, elbow, shoulder, back, shoulder, elbow: it was a dancer's sense of rhythm. Meena Kumari wore red in the publicity film with Ashok Kumar. When did white become her favourite colour, if it was her favourite?

—————

The blackness of Meena's hair was more noticeable than a dark complexion. Was Ashok Kumar the biggest star of Bombay films in 1953, as claimed? How long was it before Dilip displaced him?

—————

Would Gene Kelly rather have danced with Shah Rukh Khan than Sinatra? Best of all would have been dancing with Karishma Kapoor.

—————

As they sang to celebrate the doll's wedding, the effortless high notes were reassuring. 'The moon is still the same", its intimacy comparable with Brel's "Jojo" or Françoise Hardy at her best, confirmed to my ear the identity of the singer. Shekhar pictures them garlanding each other, then a train is superimposed on his study. Did Kamal Amrohi think of that when a speeding train at night disturbs Pakeezah's repose? How long did Amrohi survive Meena Kumari? Guru Dutt's widow was dead within two years (or just over).

Did E. M. Forster have no contact with the class of Bengalis described in "Parineeta"? They are an equivalent of the gentry in Jane Austen, Turgenev, even Proust's Marcel and his family. There is no mention of the British or independence movements or Western technology, apart from the train, which is taken for granted.

Bimal Roy was city-born, like Scheherezade, in his case, in Dacca. Did he feel bitter towards the landowning class because his own family had lost most of its property? The rich landowner in "Parineeta" has made his money in sugar. Does he own extensive lands outside Calcutta? The rich and poor Brahmins are both dead by the end; the future is with the rich, energetic man of lower caste (more refined than the new man in 'The Cherry Orchard") and Shekhar, the cultured Brahmin, a man full of curiosity. Is Shekhar, who has many interests but is impractical, a self-portrait of the novelist?

—————

Do Kashmiris have different connotations of blue because so many have blue eyes?

—————

Bluer Than Oxalis

The first two L. P. s of Françoise Hardy were solid, matching the craftsmanship of the recordings; the third was thinner, as though popular music no longer required quality.

―――――

The first announcement was: the umpire is a Frenchwoman; I did not quite make out the score. I was reminded of Rainer's saying that a French accent in English is unmistakeable.

―――――

Samiya wore an indigo gown, more becoming than the black worn by some women teachers. Just after Veer's renunciation, a phrase from Lata shocks like Shane Warne spinning the ball from outside leg stump to hit off when thought no longer capable of doing so.

―――――

After the bleak 'eighties and early 'nineties, Lata could be light-hearted again.

―――――

"Salaam, Salman. Is your name a variant of Solomon?"
 "Of course. My wisdom was predicted. My family had a first-rate astrologer. We weren't nobodies."

―――――

Colin, my landlord, said: "When the Beatles sing 'Twist and Shout', they make you want to twist; other singers don't." Even at sixty-seven, Lata is more rhythmic than Udit Naryan.

―――――

Certain stripes are pleasing; other stripes are not. Do beautiful people have patterns of D. N. A. that are pleasing to the eye? Who decides on the pigmentation that appears on the computer screen? Is there a typical pattern for a great composer and another for a great painter?

―――――

Imagine a troll named Erroll;
That would give a new slant on a troll.
He would down alcohol by the bucket
But it would take a fearful toll.
Looking twenty years older than he was—
Much like the worked-out Boz—
He would sigh for the lover's role
But drink took a fearful toll.

―――――

Shah Rukh Khan and Karishma Kapoor—charisma and Karishma.

―――――

Mihir Bose says that Americans and British are incapable of empathising with dark-skinned people. Americans would only accept the very fair-skinned Isabelle Adjani, dubbed.

―――――

There was a touch of Valentino about Shah Rukh Khan when he was saying: "Closer! Closer!" to Madhuri Dixit.

―――――

Shane Warne's signature baffled me in its flight. How did he get an elaborate capital out of -ne?

─────

"You were a bit of a Shah Rukh Khan in that film: playing the violin, kissing a girl's hand—with such a flourish."
"I like your hair," said Susan; "in the film," she added by way of explanation. Still, it was half a compliment the centre parting had earned me. Whose idea was it? Storer's? Charlie Forster's?

─────

Vincent Cronin writes that Napoleon's tactics remained unchanged and his enemies became used to them, but he won twelve of his last fourteen battles.

─────

"I don't know what's going on," said Bernard Cornwell. "Napoleon has more voltigeurs than men in his column; the column is a feint; German craftsmen from Pennsylvania have updated his rifles; sharpshooters from the woods of France and the forests of America are decimating my men every two hours. He even has Mongol horsemen and—a dastardly dart this—Sharpe was deceived by the Comanche wheel: braves clinging to the far side of apparently riderless horses—a stratagem known to the readers of boys' comics but not, alas, Sharpe. He looks like a pin-cushion now. I'll have to take refuge among my Irish-American and Hispanic-American readers."
(C. S. Forester's "Death to the French" is about a Rifleman who is cut off from his unit in the retreat through Portugal. It draws on the recollections of Rifleman Harris.)

─────

Was Metternich always a cold-hearted seducer, applying realpolitik in the bedroom?

─────

The place where smallminded clerics bedevilled Bach's career was the place where Napoleon was brought down by the forces of absolutism.

"If the country's too monotonous to give scope to Napoleon, it's not much good for artists. Bach would have been better off in Dresden."

─────

Napoleon should have played his natural game, like Adam Gilchrist. His best chance of defeating Wellington without sustaining heavy casualties was a battle of manoeuvre. He was overconfident, assuming that the Prussians had been mauled and could not fight another battle so soon. Logically, Grouchy and his thirty thousand men were available to outflank Wellington, whose men were behind the brow of a hill, so suffered few casualties from artillery fire. (Shells landed on mud, which deadened their impact.) They would be exposed to fire from their left flank. Six thousand men could be detached to launch a second outflanking attack farther back. Many of Wellington's men would panic. Napoleon would be attacking Wellington's left flank three or four hours before the first Prussians could attack his right flank. It would have been a characteristic Napoleonic battle.

─────

Might Napoleon, in time of peace, have become a nose?

─────

Bluer Than Oxalis

Andrew Motion's unwonted inertia
Threatened the motion that snubs to Persia
Should be construed as a casus belli
Against the benighted minister, Ruth Kelly,
Who fancies herself as a bit of a Grace Kelly.
(She may be a Papist but not in a state of grace.)
Motion's no Heseltine, wielding the mace;
He's a Poet Laureate, who knows his place
For all that he dotes on Nelson.
Put Kelly in a half-Nelson, dress her in a stetson
And nothing else. "You're a bit wet, son,"
Nelson might have said to Motion, scorning his emotion,
Scorning his qualms. "I'm not in search of alms,"
Said Motion. "I want a proper sinecure.
There's nothing like the lure of a proper sinecure."

―――――

A screenplay: Al Quaeda operatives plot to sabotage the Israeli nuclear research establishment. A moderate Moslem finds out and warns them that the repercussions will be far-ranging. They are determined to go ahead. Mossad realises that something is going on. There is love interest between a noble English teacher and a beautiful Persian / Lebanese woman. (Why not both?) The plot is foiled but the research establishment, which has not been supervised by the Knesset for fifty years, still blows up. The disaster is worse than Chernobyl, worse than Pompeii and Herculaneum; people flee to the desert, the sea, to Iraq. The Holy Places become inaccessible.

―――――

"Great Britain," said Lara; an arrestingly rare phrase in London television nowadays.

―――――

"Fatties of 'The Times', led by Mary Anne Sieghart, Libby Purves and Caitlin Moran, are taking on ballerinas of the Maryinsky, St. Petersburg to prove themselves fitter."

She can wield a machete can Shilpa Shetty
If left on the jetty when there are prizes to be won.
She's no put-upon Pushpa of "Amar Prem";
She's more like a member of the crême de la crême,
Running her boss—if necessary—in to the ground
And climbing the ladder two rungs at a time,
Wrongs without reason or rhyme nothing to her.

"What was it like stacking bobbins of cotton while sales representatives came through the workshop who weren't as well qualified as you?"
    "Galling."

Scarlett Johanneson visits Venice each year. Is the city reflected in her face? Philip Howard visits Florence each year to see 'The Birth of Venus'. How often does he go to Venice?
    "Are you a Venus sort of chap?"

London's turned on Bambi;
Shaka's Ama-Wombe
Could not be more cruel,
Broad blades stabbing in place
Of quill pens—no elegant

Bluer Than Oxalis

Satire here. The mill-race
Becomes a maelstrom, Tony
Drowning in Old Red ink, his font
Of New Labour become a sink
Of iniquity. And whose fault?
Tony's. No-one went along with him.
He multiplied himself in Commons divisions.
Now he's out on his ear like a football
Manager, con man found out,
Shopped by his accomplices,
Who'll be there for years to come.

―――――

We are the telebores;
We're not so pretty as hellebores;
We're not so bright as hellebores;
But we're great at boring the hell out of people.
We know it riles when we talk about our carbon miles,
Flying to Laos and telling others not to.
We glory in our riling, we always come back smiling
From our trips to Laos. We're not Laos-Wowsers,
We're carbon-wowsers, recycling programmes—
You've only heard about global warming three thousand times
But we said it first, we pretend. Of all
The Jehovah's Witnesses in all the world
You had to get us in your living-room.
That is your doom: to live at the same time as us.
Recycle, recycle, any old cycle, any old telly—
You think? Why not a peep about digital waste?
Because the B. B. C. makes money out of waste.
Bo-Peep has more savvy than the B. B. C..

―――――

Brown's not a man for folderols.
I doubt if he's one for Parker Knolls
But assuredly for taxes and tolls.

─────

"Having slandered people who say negro," said David Cameron, "I've noticed that, in Romance languages, words denoting blackness begin with -n, so I'm banning Romance languages in co-operation with America. Anyone speaking those languages will be taken to Guantanamo Bay and shrunk, using the latest technology." (or stretched, using sixteenth century technology.)

─────

Lara's "jolly" suggested a higher class upbringing than her diction might.

─────

He was happily choosing the music for his funeral.

─────

Iranian women don't think much of Arab patterns, preferring Turkish and their own.
    "If you don't think much of Arabs, why do you think that Allah chose to speak to an Arab?"
    "Out of the goodness of His heart."

─────

The English gentleman is admired everywhere but England.

─────

Bluer Than Oxalis

There's no malarkey
At Issey Miyake,
No soap-box spouting,
No tabloid pouting.
There's a fragrance for Saki
At Issey Miyake,
Cool and poised—
A whiff of the cruel?
No, this is urbane,
Not Alistair McLean,
But Saki at Issey Miyake.
(I've never tried it.)

─────

"I feel an initiative coming on," said Tony Blair.
   "Lie down. You'll soon feel better."

─────

Jicky is said to be the cologne of Napoleon, more likely an attempt to approximate to it. If Brel's Jacky had worn Jicky, would it have improved his morale?

─────

Listening to "Sous le Pont Mirabeau", Rainer commented on the peculiar melancholy of French songs. Rainer was long-winded; John thought him boring and was curt; yet, in some ways, Rainer was more sensitive than John. Rainer thought that northern Germans were like the English, whereas southern Germans had more in common with the French.
   An ex-soldier remarked: 'The French are better at a requiem.'

─────

Heliotrope & Hansie

'That Frenchman is murdering a beautiful Jewish folk song,"
complained John, hearing "Donna, Donna". He seemed to hold me
personally responsible for all French sins.

Matilda did not know the tilde,
Though she knew the circumflex.
She may have heard of Posh and Becks,
Shallow as Scott Fitzgerald's Zelda,
But had no time for Hollywood wrecks
Nor did she want to be an Isolde,
Rather to fill the void left by Bec's
Going, Lleyton-linked, not to the orient,
But to Wimbledon, in south-west one.

Burbling on, blathering on,
Barker always blathering on—
Chief Barker's toasts could not be more tedious—
Hark to me, Barker, there'll never be larks
While you are always blathering on.
People who can speak are in a lather;
They'd rather be in Philadelphia
Than listening to Barker blathering on.
Federer's equalled Borg again, he's equalled
Borg a hundred times, and just to be sure,
You've got it between the ears, here
Is Barker blathering on.

'The blubberbutt seat was introduced so that, if aeroplanes were over-
laden, they could jettison a blubberbutt over the ocean or the Rockies.

Bluer Than Oxalis

Objections have been made that a blubberbutt might land on an elk and do it an injury. The controversy has become international because millionaire Michael Moore is flying all over the world, burning up carbon miles like cigarettes. European countries and many in Asia seek the protection of the blubberbutt seat but are worried about where Michael Moore will come down next. It has been suggested that pilots should have an internationally recognised certificate in blubberbutt ejection safety—over uninhabited areas, preferably not those containing endangered species, bearing in mind that blubberbutt ejection must sometimes be a priority."

―――――

Life loured on Lowry for a time.

―――――

Not sharing Eagleton's aversion,
I'll change my rhyme from Arabic to Persian,
Which would gladden the heart of Waldemar,
Who swooned in Stamboul but dotes on Persian
Art, challenging the Judaeo-Christian version
Of history, saying the East is all slavery.
Yet bridges from East to West are built
On the arch, not the pillar. What a bravery
Of coloured wisdom adorns
The walls of the finest mosques.

―――――

Percy's more of a saint than Bernard,
Would never fight with red-hot pokers,
Is cool in a team who are never chokers,
Exults in the trophies they have garnered
And, no doubt, had a whale of a time

Without drinking himself to oblivion.
It's a valley of tears for Jonny after four years on the heights;
Dips are there to be jumped out of.
Did Montgomery come over with the Conqueror?
This Montgomery came over with the conqueror.
John Smit, indomitable as Christian de Wet,
Can play on the veld or in the wet,
Can burrow or leap, though others leap higher;
He has Victor Matfield to inspire,
Stultify the English, arouse their ire,
Douse their fire, control the set-piece,
Leave them in the mire.
Kick for goal when in range and, when out of range,
Call on Francois Steyn to rewrite range,
Without losing sense of reason or rhyme,
Without making alcohol a lime
For the wits, as do some nitwits.
Springboks are bucking, rather mauling than rucking.

―――――

"We murdered them," said John Inverdale. "We beat them to the last sandwiches in the canteen. How can they stand the humiliation of being beaten to the last sandwiches in the canteen?"

―――――

Crowing English cricket,
Neither crow nor cricket,
Neither fish nor fowl,
You'll never be Martin Crowe,
You'll never be Glenn McGrath.
You're not even la-di-da
These days, nor bucolic,
Just acerbic. Justin Langer

Bluer Than Oxalis

Could teach you what passion is.
You take a prang as you did
When Jeff Thomson went: "Whang"
And you whinge. When you win,
You are insufferable.
(A response to Inverdale and the general drunken complacency; 2007)

─────

When, Jane Shilling, did four Mitfords play Test cricket for Pakistan? When were three Mitfords mothers of Pakistan cricket captains? When did three become famous singers? And what about the Bach family?

─────

An Oxford accent need not be so strained as a Mitford accent.
   'They mocked each other's accent.'
   'That's taking the gloves off.'

─────

He's a lesser Andrew, Motion,
And not so merry as Andrew Marvell.
Does Motion dream that a potion
Could turn him in to a genius, like Marvell?

─────

My mother pointed out that, when people of working class origin get on, there is usually someone of higher class not many generations back. Carol Vorderman's father left when she was a few weeks old and her mother was poor but her paternal great-grandfather was chief medical officer in the Dutch East Indies and another great-grandfather was a prosperous butcher in Prestatyn.

─────

"I was up and down like a yo-yo, boyo.
I got up; they knocked me down; I got up; they knocked me down.
Unpronounceable? They're unplayable.
My bruises look like a tattoo in the shape of Fiji.
The red dragon wanted to breathe fire
But it didn't have the legs to breathe it in the right place
And it couldn't fly; any self-respecting dragon flies.
Gareth Edwards and Gerald Davies were dragons who flew.
This was one of the days when Dagon, the Philistine god,
Bested the chapel—or perhaps we had too much of the pub
And not enough of the chapel."

—————

Spanish journalists report that Barcelona has bought the Taj Mahal, having made Agra an offer it could not refuse. Barcelona will also bring to Spain Versailles and Chartres cathedral. Madrid is negotiating the purchase of Hagia Sophia and the best bits of St. Petersburg. The Madrid motto is: we have ways to make you sell.

—————

Dodi is dead as the dodo, Mohammed.
Mohammed is with us like Frodo, Mohammed.
Hardy's Elfride counts more than Al Fayed.
The world is more tired of Al Fayed than Elfride,
Who still has a reader or two, but Al Fayed
Is mired in delusion, which turns people off,
And is his shop, Harrods, the place for a toff?
He may be direct but as strong as Joe Roff?
A naiad is sweeter than a "Life of Pi" ed.
We put up with David Miliband but why Ed?

Chapter Six

Misadventure On A Bean-stalk

Scene 1: "I was playing Jack and I was climbing the bean-stalk but it just kept on going: so did I: and I came out in a strange-looking place, not far from a brook—above the stage?—and in front of an imposing house. Some actors see ghosts. I must be having hallucinations, I thought. I started descending the bean-stalk, the play fell in to place; and, when I asked the rest of the cast afterwards, I found I had only been away for a few seconds, no longer than usual."

"Which performance was that?"

"Evening. Next time nothing happened. Then came the matinée. I went on climbing—and I found myself beside a chimney, with a ladder leading down in to it, and I felt annoyed with my subconscious. Why wasn't it logical? Why did I not see the same things as last time? I began descending the ladder—and I was back on stage. But I felt I was somewhere else at the same time if I could only concentrate. Was I ever going to meet the giant? When I met one in our company, he was a let-down."

"Were you level with the gods?"

"It seemed that I was above the gods, climbing ever higher. And red bean flowers were beautiful—now I remember... the chimney was decorated with bean flowers."

"A bean-stalk's not Everest; you can't get altitude sickness. They do say that actors never quite know what world they're in."

Scene 2: "I timed you from the moment you began climbing the bean-stalk."

"My time was different. I was descending the ladder while you were still watching me climbing and, when I got to the bottom, there was someone so big I could only see him up to the knees and I didn't want to see any more, so I climbed up the chimney while you could see me descending the bean-stalk—and I took up the play where I left off."

"How much longer will the play run?"

"Two and a half weeks."

"You can go a long way in that time."

Scene 3: "How did it go? You look as though pantomime's wearing you down."

"My hands were sweating as I climbed the bean-stalk. My time seemed to jump from the roof to the hearth. There was a great foot on a stool, which was almost as high as my head. The foot was as long as my leg, longer."

"You came down helter-skelter."

"I came down even more helter-skelter in my dream, in my other life, in whatever on earth it is, or out of earth it is—he was chasing me and, if he had got his range, I should have been skewered with a fork, then, in his range, he threw his pipe at me—it was longer than a golf club, it could have been an organ-pipe, but, luckily, it missed."

Scene 4: "That giant's in my head day and night now, waking or sleeping."

"How do you climb the bean-stalk in your dreams—the same way as on stage?"

"I'm light as a feather in my dreams. I'm not even aware of climbing. There were several sweet peas all about the mantelpiece—in reality, or rather, when I had slid out of this life in to another. Somehow a giant who likes flowers seems less dreadful—but were they his flowers? Had they bounded forth from my imagination? Who else was up there?

"Your mezzanine in the sky must be getting familiar by now. It's all in your head really. You're taking the part too seriously, dreaming about it and carrying your dreams in to performance."

Misadventure On A Bean-stalk

"I wish I were so sure. I'm awake on stage yet you say I'm dreaming. There's another worry. They've changed the script. I have to carry the heroine up the bean-stalk. They wanted me to take her up to the giant's castle..."

'What giant's castle? I haven't seen one."

'There isn't one; we're doing it on the cheap. The snag is, if I'm carrying the heroine, I'm liable to drop her in a third universe; she'll never be seen again; only I can't say that. Directors! The run's going to be cut short, which suits me."

Scene 5: 'That was a donnybrook with a dash of Jackie Chan. I've never seen a fight look so real on stage. The audience loved it. The giant got a big hand. I wondered why he didn't take a curtain-call."

"Neither of them did. I was in the wings with the heroine, relieved that we'd both come through it safely, when the giant, the actor giant, came from the direction of his dressing-room—he'd had trouble with his stilts; he couldn't get his trousers on over them—then I looked on stage and there he was gone, the real giant, the one from God knows where, so I grabbed the heroine and rushed her on for a curtain-call. I'm glad it's all over."

"And nothing remains?"

'This coin. It's not giant-size; it could be gold—more likely fool's gold; but it's odd. It looks ancient. You don't find such things on stage every day."

"Will you take it to the British Museum?"

"Probably. I'm nervous about what they might tell me. One thing I'm sure about. I'll never play Jack again."

(Jean Gimpel wrote that the twelfth century was full of beans. Was "Jack and the Bean-stalk" made up then or later?)

─────

O Earthling, O Ashling, who write about most anything and
    sprinkle errors everywhere
As though your necklace were undone, the Althing would not
    welcome you.
O Ashling, O Earthling, Edgar Atheling and Ethelred and Edward,
    never thought so dread
As William, vacillated—but did they lie
As Ashling, plugged in a parlous lie,
Trying to square her notions. Emotions
Are for the backward Hindus, who eat laddoos
Far from London and count themselves lucky
Not to be at a media party. Hearties
At a party hurt the soul.
("unnecessary songs")

―――――

Ashling O'Connor was fuming. No-one had sworn at her in the lift; no-one had elbowed her aside. How could she be gritty and modern if people weren't gritty and modern about her? Was Hugo Rifkind daring to smile at her? she asked herself as she stalked through the open plan office to the sensible part with her own space—and he tried to keep up with her. Did he think he was a soldier? And why was he called Hugo? The rat-tat-tat of her questions settled on this point. Wasn't he supposed to be Estonian-Jewish-Scottish and yet he had persuaded his parents to name him Hugo, like a mediaeval French knight. Why couldn't he have a plain, down-to-earth name, like Ashling? She seethed at the impudence of that Estonian-Jewish-Scottish baby.

"Happy Valentine's Day," cried Hugo—and then had the impudence to give her nothing. Speaking to her, not speaking to her, not even giving her a box of chocolates so that she could become fat, like Sieghart and Purves, and merit promotion: was there no end to his cheek?

And then it dawned on her that there was a reason for this

unwonted passion. She was tough as old boots. Then along came Hugo, an ordinary hack.

─────

"Are you picking on the poor woman because of her name?"
   "No. She's probably not related to O'Connor the evil."

─────

Ashling O'Connor thinks it novel for a Bombay star to play an alcoholic. Dilip Kumar in "Devdas" (1955) and Guru Dutt in "Kaagaz ke Phool" (1959) did so long ago, Shah Rukh Khan in the remake of "Devdas". 'Teen Deewarein' ('Three Walls"), in which Naseeruddin Shah plays a Hyderabadi baddie, includes a few brutal scenes in prison, which might be to the taste of American and British television people, but the twist at the end is reminiscent of 'forties Hollywood, a more fruitful influence. Nagesh Kukunoor was a chemical engineer in America for five years. America has rubbed off on him. Have the chemicals too? Does he talk like an engineer rather than a typical middle class Hyderabadi? He made a call-centre manager the protagonist of his first film (hardly a hero).

> Hyderabad blues are like Hollywood blues and then some.
> The call-centre entrepreneur must juggle his twosome,
> His cock-and-hen sum of two careers, two identities,
> Rival aspirations—and make the 'phone lines hum.

─────

"Veer-Zaara" is a typical great Bombay film; "Hum Turn" has the warmth of "Cheers" at its best, with good songs (and Rani Mukherji has a wider range as an actress than Shelley Long); "Dil To Paga Hai" is joyous, the best film of its kind I've seen, except that I'm not sure I've seen another film of its kind. "Hum Turn" is a genuine romantic comedy, romantic and funny, like the Australian 'The Dead Letters Office". What an impoverished existence these people lead who know only degenerate Hollywood.

Ritwik Ghattak's "Cloud-capped Star" is probably the most perfect tragedy of Indian cinema, quiet, poignant, beautiful. It is like Turgenev and Alain-Fournier, with no false note. Great Bombay films tend to be Dickensian or Shakespearean.

"Sholey"
Lovely in her mourning white, Radha added a more spiritual radiance to the festival of colours, a soft light to dusk; the plaintive mouth-organ tune seemed to answer her face, appeal to it, reach out to her sorrow, hinting that loneliness yearning could lift loneliness from her heart. It was a tune that came from roving yet a tune played only for her, among all the women's faces the player had looked upon; he chose to serenade her in the night. Grave she remained to the end, but she had begun to quicken within as he had begun to sway in the first dance steps until her face caught his eye, so her heart had begun to respond to the first dance steps of feeling since her loss. She had thought herself bereft for life yet a man had come who would set her blood dancing again, who would not steal her jewels from a safe but would win the jewel of her love. He spoke to her through his shyness more than by many words. Did she think him a prince in blue denim?

"Isaura"
It was like a drumming on bones, her tune, yet more than a drumming, a melody expressing pent-up energy, moving only between the ordained succession of keys yet giving these a sense of boundless space. Her touch was attuned to gold thread yet here she was touching the primeval, the ancestral. It was as though a lady

had gone from embroidering tapestry to helping Leonardo with his dissections.

─────

"Why must I have an animal as a soul? Why can't I have a colour or a melody?" His soul hovered above him as musical notation. Anyone who could read music could see his soul.

─────

The neat whisky should have been a warning. Five or six teaspoonfuls she expected me to drink while talking about China. Was there any other girl I had met at school or university who took for granted such a consumption of whisky?
 "Did she put you off China for life?"
 "She put me off whisky."

─────

Kandinsky declines from his early Russian painting, with its striking mauve. Tim Marlow saw more in the paintings than most people would. His two horsemen of the apocalypse looked more like a llama to me. Mondrian's blocks of colour are meaningless, whatever Marlow may say.

─────

Leonardo was not quick on the uptake where painter's materials are concerned, failing to apply science to art. He should have gone to school to Jan van Eyck.

─────

Why should Shostakovich alone be given credit for cryptic resistance to tyranny? Prokoviev used to think: I must write a bit of rubbish here as a coded message that Stalin is getting me down. Some who talk now of Shostakovich being oppressed denied twenty-five years ago that the Soviet Union was oppressive. B. B. C. news reporters pretended that Russians could talk freely on television.

A young Dutch violinist, promoted by the B. B. C., said she likes all of Shostakovich. I don't like every sentence of Dickens, every line of Shakespeare. Shostakovich remained dissatisfied with his fourth symphony, saying parts of it were too ostentatious. I've always liked the quiet ending. Was that his favourite bit?

Indian acting includes a stylised shaking of the head as in the scenes involving Anandi and her maidservant, whose shaking is villainous, perhaps intended to recall a snake. At other times, the shaking is deferential, accompanying a salaam. Anandi walked with chest thrust out, a slight imperious wobble of the breasts demanding obeisance to her womanhood as well as to the wife of the future Peshwa.

Jumuna's ear-rings were little tea-cosies of pearls. Raana Khan has never seen a diamond yet so many people around him wear a profusion of pearls. Divers must have been busy in Indian waters. Ahilya, though in mourning, wears two or three strings of golden pearls. Raghoba and the Peshwa each have a red spot inside a red oblong (not filled in). Mahadji's oblong is vertical. "I think the men get a raw deal with forehead markings." Jumuna has a gondola between her eyes. The only swastika or fylfot so far was behind Mahadji and Jumuna when they were reunited. The former water-carrier had been given a basket of blessed sweets which also contained bills of exchange wrapped around cylinders like piano-rolls or batons. Ahilya, so the moneylenders said, had paid off Mahadji's debts. She commanded Mahadji to write hymns as interest on the money she had lent him.

Misadventure On A Bean-stalk

"A person, while seeming nothing, can be everything," said Ahilya to the woman through whom she gave Mahadji five hundred thousand rupees.

Kartika Rane's sari was mainly red, trimmed with gold. Her nose-clip was of pearls, set in silver. She looked wifely, standing, rather than seductive as when she lay on her side. Jumuna sang of Krishna stealing her clothes as she bathed in the river Jumuna. She had remembered Mahadji's words which had slipped his memory. Was he in truth a songwriter? Robert Clive is depicted as dignified, astute, fluent in Bengali, well-versed in Indian politics. He had recognised the pre-eminent talents of Mahadji Scindia before anyone else. Is this true? Clive is no more a free agent than Mahadji. He has to satisfy the directors of the Company. Mahadji sets great store by his feudal loyalty to the Peshwa.

Deadly, dagger-throwing eunuchs provided an original touch of black humour.

─────

Mahadji was in the thick of the fray; the Peshwa sat it out astride his charger. Knobs of metal on leather patches made the Peshwa's dress more warlike. Raghoba took refuge in the hubble-bubble from the brabble about him. Anandi stopped her maid from showering him with flowers. Mahadji pleaded for clemency towards Raghoba and was then applauded for pardoning the fake Jankoji.

─────

Sally's front niggled me. "Love"? "Live"? Why then was the second letter a diamond of dots like dice on dominoes, neither "O" nor "I"? Was Sally saying—or her designer saying—that love is a lottery, life is a lottery, so have fun and wear pretty clothes? Sally would have enjoyed wearing a domino and mask at a Venetian carnival. Her smock had a black ground the colour of night, the word, whatever it was, with a flower in the "L", like illumination in a manuscript,

was in the colour of revels—and Sally was in a mood for revels.
   (I like the melody.)

—————

Brian Johnston: Mark Waugh is having his innings edited by a young lady from his sponsor, who'll be coming on at the end of the over for a discussion. We've given her a mike, and that should add extra colour.
Amanda: I think, Mark, we'll have to cut out those edgy strokes on the third and fifth balls.
Mark Waugh: You mean those leg glances for two. They were intended.
Amanda: I know you like to think you're in control. I've soothed many an artist. Even if, as you say, you intended to hit them down there, we can't be too clever for the spectators, can we? I suggest that we play through the V—that's thought very sound; ask Trevor Bailey—but—this I must stress—to increase your earnings potential and become one of our first rank clients, you ought to hit some sixes straight and over that way (waving vaguely towards square leg). And you could grow a beard like Ian Botham. He's shaved it off but he had one in his prime. And I'd really like button-flies and turn-ups, at least as an idea to toss around.
Mark Waugh: The bowler's waiting.
Amanda: Oh, I am sorry. (Jogs off slowly with a show of hurry.)
Brian Johnston: That was a lovely, wristy stroke through mid-on by Mark Waugh. No.. .not again. The ball's gone out of shape. There's a conference. Both umpires have examined it.. .and Mark Waugh's editor is on the field again. She's examining the ball. She wants it changed. She's certainly punctuating the innings.
Bill Frindall: Dotting the "i"s and crossing the "t"s.
Trevor Bailey: To my mind, she's one luxury the game can do without. Is she going to decide what sort of sandwiches he can eat?
Brian Johnston: By the look of her, she could well be picking out a claret.

Misadventure On A Bean-stalk

Bill Frindall: That's actionable.
Trevor Bailey: Hardly. I think she's hoping to be one of Wisden's five editors of the year.
Brian Johnston: You've made it up. You thought I'd fall for that one, Boil.
Trevor Bailey: I did make it up, but it's only a matter of time before there is an award. If players are decked out with advertisements, anything's possible.

Robert Thomson of 'The Times" should take his staff on a works outing to the cemeteries of Verdun to see French cowardice.

In some Iranian villages, it is not usual to give the names of women and girls to strangers; a few miles away, the custom is different. Kiarostami is making the point that the current customs in Teheran need not apply everywhere for all time. I saw a woman in Blackburn covered in black from head to toe. (And in Nottingham on two occasions.) The women in 'Through the Olive Trees" wore white hoods, the girl's showing an inviting fringe of hair. A feminist film director wore a token blue scarf over the top of her head. Acting, she wore a hood of four or five colours.

Kiarostami's films are thoughtful, seemingly austere yet quickly engrossing, like Bach keyboard music. "Where is the Friend's House?" reminds me of Truffaut's "Les Quatre Cent Coups" (The Four Hundred Blows"). Mohsen Mahalbat's "A Moment of Innocence" is playful yet profound, again like Truffaut, this time "Day For Night". 'The Rose" has the same palette as her father's film but without the romance and beauty of imagery.

Heliotrope & Hansie

Louis de Bernières likes racial stereotypes. He should consider the smiling Iranian cleric explaining that a Shia temporary marriage can last half an hour or a thousand years.

―――――

To the British food industry, the number of the Beast is not 666 but three and a half per cent fibre, moist.

―――――

"Make way for me," said Libby Purves. "I'm an opinion-former."

―――――

Doff your hat to Schaffer.
Many a scientist would call him gaffer.
His students thought his notions a jaffa.
Offa's Dyke was not such a mark, deep
In his students' consciousness.
And yet they found his lectures a lark.
(I remember Simon Schaffer on "University Challenge", He was bright.)

―――――

Did Jimmy Porter drink Piesporter
While railing as he didn't oughta,
Nailing a decade for Tynan, tying
Logic in knots for a more detached view?
No. He'd want something stronger than porter
Or Piesporter. His jaws were a gin-trap,
Snapping on boozy class-struggle.
What a slew of Aunt Sallys he sought to slay
But most of them lived to bore another day

Misadventure On A Bean-stalk

"Look back in anger"?
They know more of Wenger in Stavanger
Than Osborne's railing, stiff as a hangar.
Wenger has no doppelgänger
Nor has Ferguson a double.

―――――

'Tessa Jowell was a magnificent name for last year but this year is this year and it's time for a new name. Cleopatra has been suggested, since she has worked hand-in-glove with Tony."

―――――

A fillip is a blow, not a carrot. Losing the Ashes will give a fillip to Australian cricket.

―――――

Would Australian Pinot Noir taste more like Australian Shiraz then Burgundian Pinot Noir because of its terroir?

―――――

Mark well, Clarke. General Mark Clark
Was top-dog for a time, now
Is despised for his vanity-drive
To Rome. You may strive to shuffle
Off responsibility, appear unruffled,
Say: "What a kerfuffle over nothing."
It is not nothing.
(Charles Clarke, Home Secretary)

―――――

Lulu never met a Zulu.
Like Benaud, he might have thought her a Lulu,
That Zulu, who missed out.

─────

"Michel Ney chewed tobacco and commanded the rearguard on the retreat from Moscow. Twenty National Health Service propagandists will set out from Moscow in winter, wearing uniforms of the early nineteenth century, and will walk to Germany or Austria, depending on their navigation. Each week viewers will vote on the medical expert they want put out of his or her misery. The winner will receive ten years' private medical insurance."
   (I've never smoked.)

─────

"Oh, Benazir, you're as deadly as Benayoun, mysterious as the Mountains of the Moon; when I hear you, I'm not myself; I forget to sneer. And my sneer is as famous as the Cheshire cat's grin. I'm not from Cheshire. I'm from all over the place—and I feel all over the place when I see you, when I hear you, when I touch you—and how you touch me. The biggest trout in the most secret pool of Patagonia responds to your pheromones. Swear that you do not love Esler; swear that you do not love Crick. They say that he is so softened that his amorous feelings for you are spreading like an oil-slick."

─────

When Benazir Bhutto left office in 1996, Pakistan was one of the most corrupt countries in the world; now, in 2007, it is forty-three places off the bottom. Since 1999, the Pakistan economy has grown nearly as quickly as India's. A third of local councillors must be women; there is a quota of women in parliament.

─────

Misadventure On A Bean-stalk

Will President Musharraf send photogenic agitators to plunge the B. B. C. and News International in to anarchy?

\-\-\-\-\-

Before I went to 'nam,
I was virtuous as Rama.
I came back numb from 'nam
But I made my name in 'nam
And could have found a home in my name.
(not about John McCain but written after hearing him discussed)

\-\-\-\-\-

I remember Susan sunlit, with a rhododendron in her hair, smiling on the edge of an argument—about politics—the sun bathed in her cheeks like an infusion of liquid in a cocktail, adding and heightening, and overhead willow trees with their memories of Ophelia and Desdemona.

\-\-\-\-\-

"Speedwell," said Susan, in answer to my unspoken question. I regarded it happily, comparing the blue of the flower with the shade of her eyes, instinctively feeling this was a moment to treasure, her hand—which seemed to glow in the sun—was Chinese art in a nutshell. The image came to me, the way that Gray would phrase it, and how it would bound forth in its glory as eternal truth can always transcend the lips of a fool. This was one of the days that fill the hive of memory. A day when fate is magnanimous.

\-\-\-\-\-

Dowland's themes unfolded endlessly, like Ariadne's thread which never gave out but led on in to the blackness of despair and out again to the light.

―――――

It suddenly struck him that the world is worlds, that each of us knows as much of his neighbour's lives as Robin Hood of the hideout of the Assassins.

―――――

It was a land of hedges and diving hollows that made me want to hide and play at ambush. Here a thoughtful child could ramble afar, snug in his own psyche.

―――――

Rita kept unzipping her trousers absently, revealing as she did so white knickers adorned with flowers.
    "I like your flowers," I observed. Smiling, she waited a space, then nonchalantly closed her zip.

―――――

George is right and Bill is wrong and the wrong one you have
    chose.
I'll go where the girls are pretty and still the nose of Cyrano for
    one who knows is next the rose.
Clinton for changes and yet, when he's ensconced, you'll find him
    a changeling president who's intent on just one thing,
Massaging figures and his face so he'll look good in the books.
But all these promises will fly back home, you can't fit a free range
    beneath a dome, the geese are cackling on the Capitol but
    not to give a warning.

Misadventure On A Bean-stalk

Clinton is for growth and he says he's for apple pie
But a Democrat Jack Homer will pick plums for a lobbying guy.

"I saw your angelic feet" went to her heart
And made her feet itch to learn the art
Of her ancestors far from Derby. Meena danced
On glass and the blood was the blood of all
Her ancestors, pulsing to the same rhythms
Age after age, as much a dream time
As the Dreamtime of the Aborigines.
To be rescued by a snake, to be rescued by an elephant,
By a hero—that was living, that was dreaming
In a land where dreams, as always, are necessary
To life as in England—but topdogs deny it.
(A double danced on glass, writes Mihir Bose.)

As Chloë warmed to her subject and got in to her stride, she remembered that Jack was liable to find her boring. But he was beginning to see the sex appeal of the Depression when it suffused her face with enthusiasm.

Wodehouse's wit danced like a butterfly amid the blooms and bloomers of Broadway.

"I want a badge," cried Charlotte, childlike in her thirst for a new toy. She was sitting closer to me than in the office, giving me the chance to examine her jewellery. Little pearl ear-rings, clasped on the lobe, supplemented by pendant ear-rings. What I had carelessly thought was a brooch was a pendant between her delightfully adumbrated breasts. There was a cameo on the pendant, I think. Was it perchance a locket after all, containing a picture of someone she loved? No, it was merely a cameo, I decided. She wore her usual array of rings and bangles, numerous as those of an African woman, but also the single green jade ring which stood out from the rest.

―――――

The daintiness of her pearl ear-rings matched her face when boldness deserted her and the world seemed suddenly more than she could manage. There was something vulnerable about those pearls.

―――――

Clive is a windbag at heart
But he thinks he is custodian
Of all the winds, his art
More than wordplay
For television or "The Guardian".
Keats he extols and Pushkin too
And hopes to enrol his name
Among the great as though
He had taken five wickets at Lord's.

―――――

"A floozy on an Apaloosa came my way," said Steve Martin. "I could not bear to lose her, so I followed that Apaloosa."

"Are you only in key with California or with universities all over the U.S.A. ?"

"I chime here; I chime there. Sometimes it takes a Quasimodo to ring the bell, sometimes I can be subtle. I love being subtle but the world conspires against it. I'm not a sledgehammer sort of guy, not by nature, but what the audience wants the audience... or penury. ..or another career. I've wisecracked a fault in the earth beneath Hollywood—the whole place would fall through a crack or a wisecrack. A journey to the centre of the earth, or, at least, nether California—not lower California; that's south, but nether California, where the weather is very nether. Your garments stick to you like nobody's business and you're looking up, up, up to the Rockies. The mines of Mona are not so deep as Hollywood, gone down the plughole. I like to look fate in the face: we're doomed sooner or later.

Dan Maskell: It's a good scene when they're both playing well at the same time. We've had the crucial seventh scene, the last with the old actors. That was a great line Hamlet spoke over the high part of the footlights.
Virginia Wade: Oh, what a rally between Hamlet and his courtiers. He's so quick...and fast. I think it's done an awful lot for Nottingham, this stage, which is made of the latest materials—it's state of the art—it has really put Nottingham on the map. They say it's hard on the actors' knees and ankles but they'll have to put up with that.
Dan Maskell: Most people play their poetry mixed, so they'll be able to identify with Hamlet and Ophelia. He's pressing her hard in this scene. Virginia, was it more gentlemanly in your day?
Virginia: It was more ladylike too.
Dan Maskell: Ophelia scatters flowers amid her madness—she reminds me of someone, Virginia. Rosemary, that's for remembrance. I came around the corner one day and Lili de Alvarez of Spain was lit up by the sun, playing a backhand. I've never seen anything so beautiful. It was a coup de foudre, a backhand coup de foudre. She liked playing half-volleys near the baseline. That's art. If only life were all half-volleys near the baseline.
Virginia: Hamlet is looking so vengeful. He's really focused. When it comes to it, Dan, at this level the players can all act. It depends on

how much they want the ovation. Do they believe they can get it? Hamlet has a face like a walking suit of armour. It says: hit me and your blade will bounce right back. He's positively intimidating with his—I keep saying this—his vengefulness. One Laertes said "When I go on stage with him, I avoid meeting his eyes—they're like coals of fire."
Dan Maskell: Indeed, Virginia. Lili de Alvarez' eyes, on the other hand, were like pools of fire, the setting sun—or was it the afternoon sun—she was sunshine herself, with sunlight gathering warmth from her cheeks—and her footwork was sublime—and the position of her racquet-head was as perfect as you could ever see.
Virginia: Getting back to the duel, Dan, how do you see it going?
Dan Maskell: Hamlet will win, of course. What will be interesting is to see how he wins, with conviction, with style. Will he win like a true Hamlet and prove that he merits his star billing?
Virginia: I think he's just so fast, and so... punchy.
Dan Maskell: Not punch-drunk, surely. Nor drunk. I've always heard that he deports himself like a star, that he's a credit to the stage.

─────

When Vic came for a cup of tea after supervising work on the flats below, he talked about the Australia of his youth, how a bullying wagoner had picked a quarrel with him, arranged to fight after the queue had passed the bridge, then thought better of it after seeing lean Vic heave up a sack which had fallen from his wagon. Similarly, I had been underestimated for being thin.

─────

I found hell not far from Shepherd's Bush
And, watching the rushes, always watching the rushes,
B. B. B. producers, bloated, smarmy, of twisted
Countenance, smug, forever watching the rushes,
Flickerings in their eyes, bongoes in their ears, listed

Misadventure On A Bean-stalk

Writers lauded, "Kane" canonised, Cooper's Will Kane ignored,
Will Shakespeare patronised, updated, Jarman's like whored
To their heart's content, Whitehouse baited—
Could the Grimms have foreseen such? Yet a silver spoon
Can choke, producers die of a surfeit, guilt's
Gorge would have risen at writhing buttocks,
Those foothills on Man's ascent to the summit.
Slithering tongues, public school serpents "spoon",
Do they? They paddle like the feet of a crocodile
And Johnny Weismuller turns it over and slashes.

―――――

'They've got in to the Miami police department and falsified the iris shots. Now they can infiltrate Miami as easy as pie. Not only that but the French film archive is suing the U. S. government because François Truffaut patented the iris shot. This could run and run, longer than "Mother India" in Soviet Central Asia."

―――――

Rupert of the Rhine; Rupert of Hentzau; Murdoch.

―――――

'The enormity" of Bernard Levin's intellect was a happy howler.

―――――

"Let them eat low-fat hovis," said Tony Blair as the starving
    populace gathered before him.
"Low-fat hovis is an abomination," they protested.
"Let them eat bread containing pumpkin seeds."
"Pumpkin seeds are like stones. We cannot eat them, even in the
    wilderness you have created."

"Let them eat cheap white bread, the glory of new baking."
"Cheap white bread is neither filling nor nutritious. It is hateful to the senses."
"Let them eat cake."

———

"Rupert's of the opinion that half-English, a quarter Irish, a quarter Welsh romantics haven't had their fair share of plum jobs. The E. C. will issue a directive soon but, if we get in first, we'll look the most enlightened employer in Europe. Your new boss says you have a down on some conductor he rather likes, with a Christmassy name—I've got it written down—like Saint Nicholas."

"Anything but a saint," retorted Bernard Levin, suppressing a groan. "Nicholaus Harnoncourt. He came in to the world to plague me."

'That's as may be. Measured reviews of Harnoncourt are called for." "Working for someone who likes Harnoncourt—whoever God is, He certainly has it in for the Levins."

———

Colette enjoyed the scent of tulips in April. It has been said that tulips have no scent. Have they lost it or did Colette have a keener nose than people brought up amid petrol fumes? She grew up in the Burgundian countryside in the late nineteenth century. There would not be much industry in the district.

Colette describes Chéri as gripping Léa between his knees and Léa as gripping Cheri between her strong knees. Whose knees were on the outside?

———

Pea-pulling
"Go and knock on Rita's window," said Charlie. "I'll make some tea. Tha likes it with water, doesn't tha?"

Misadventure On A Bean-stalk

"Yes. She's not speaking to me. Shouldn't you wake her?"

"I'll be making the tea. She won't mind."

I walked along the side of the house and found the clothes-prop alluded to the day before. Lifting it and feeling for the right balance, I advanced towards the bedroom window she had described, lifted the prop and gingerly knocked on the frame, not the glass. Rita's face appeared at the window. I replaced the clothes-prop and hurried back to Charlie's home, where he had a mug of tea ready, drinkable on a chill July morning. We went out to the gate. Rita came out on to the pavement in a mac, then threw it back, smiling, to reveal that she was still wearing a blue night-dress. Having brightened the morning for us, she went back inside to make ready.

"I kept thinking you were going to stop."

I had persevered through the first day and was pulling four times as fast within a few weeks.

Chapter Seven

Le Tombeau De Miles

Miles would have enjoyed the clarinet in "Love is a Many
 Splendoured Thing"
Would he have enjoyed the mood of the film,
Savoured Hong Kong, found humour in quaintness,
Itched for his double-bass to play festive figures behind the theme
 song
And then, at the last, show how mournful a double-bass can be
When it twangs from the soul? A jazz riff stands for the menace
 of Korea
Thudding behind the singing strings as the lines of a skiff can be
 metamorphosed
In to a sampan and revolution can become Cultural Revolution.
Silken cheongsam, sleek on Eurasian limbs,
Can adorn a Western drawing-room yet always speak of the East.
Did Miles have cheongsam phrases, toy llama phrases—
Shaking him back to the train from Lima to the Andes—
Notting Hill phrases, matey as carnival,
Oxford phrases when life was more gowns than frowns?
You can't be serious when you play the double-bass.
And yet he was—profound at times.
Can you ask more of a humorist?

If jade is worn long enough, it becomes the person who wears it, says Han Su-Yin, so jade worn by Jade is doubly, trebly Jade.

—————

Might Picasso have painted tree peonies and tree ponies intermingled?
   'That sounds more like James Joyce.'

—————

"Django's more my lingo than Ringo,"
Said Miles. "I can drink Somerset stingo
But, when I dine with William Rees-Mogg,
I'm at the high table, not under the table.
Music has the variety of Table Mountain's flowers
And my taste roams like a mountain goat,
Not confined to the cable car. Bizet, without voices,
Sounding natural, is one of my choices. Jazz
Singers, with their razzmatazz, are not for me—
Apart from Bessie Smith, the good Queen Bess
Of jazz, not one to drink a Bloody Mary.
The road to Orleans goes by New Orleans:
I liked jazz before I lived in France,
Though it's a close-run thing.
The road to Orleans is très lent
If you go by a roundabout route.
A fig for franglais! I like my other stuff.
I seldom muff my other stuff.
And French jazz is dear to my heart
As French food is dear to my stomach.
I was destined to be a purveyor of French
And German wines and beers as Brian
Johnston might have been in coffee and Bamber
Gascoigne might have been in tea but I slid
Backwards in to journalism. Avid

Le Tombeau De Miles

For art, I did not hanker after garrets.
I write best, well-fed but not drunk.
I observed the mediaeval buildings in Greece,
Which the Greeks choose to ignore,
And I resisted the temptation to plunge
Headlong off a cliff. I don't know why,
But French heights are comfortable;
They must know I'm a Francophile,
So they don't tug me."

—————

He studied French and German but Django is his lingo.
He doesn't like dogs in cities, so he has no weakness for the dingo.

—————

We've put the mockers on the Okkers
Like a flight of strafing Fokkers.
Hit so sweet the leather was, it might have been morocco
On the finest set of presentation Wisdens.

—————

"It's the cross I have to bear," said Peter Crouch as the ball fell wide of him and was easily cleared.

—————

Miles lived in France, Germany and America. Which marked him the most? Surely, France.
   "Jazz critic to humorist—is that going up in the world?

—————

Jude was beside himself but Noah was behind him.

—————

A white slave complained that she had been Berber'd ten times over.

—————

"Lust for activity," commented Bernd as I was going out to play tennis. I misheard him.
    "Lust for eternity?"
    "Lust for activity," he repeated. "As you like it."
    "I am the touchstone of your wit."
    "Very good," he approved as I went off to play.

—————

Suzanne Fagence-Cooper: the natural inference is that she is French, with an English husband, yet she wore no wedding-ring and I could not detect a French accent. Tony Robinson flipped a page over. Conservatrix to her finger-tips, she caught it and let it down gently. The designs owe much to heraldry. Pugin thought red appropriate to the Lords, green to the Commons. Did he think the Lords more important, therefore requiring greater dignity and richness? One shade of red seems to have been a particular favourite of Pugin. Living in Kent, Pugin must have been near to Dickens. Did they meet socially? Did Dickens ever consider asking Pugin to design a house or furniture for him?

—————

The Co-op self -puffing brochure was edited by an ethics girl.

—————

Paxman: My Benazir, you're almost like a day's fishing.
Benazir: Almost! Am I not the acme of your desires?
Esler: Desires! What's this about desires? You told me you loved me—only me.
Paxman: I'm afraid you were deceived. She's been dallying with me for two months—except that she doesn't dilly-dally. Incidentally, who told you we'd be here?
Esler: Emily.
Paxman: That's odd. How did she know?
Benazir: But she's faithful to me. My charisma has bewitched her. She would never tell one of my lovers about another... unless... she were jealous.
Paxman: You mean...?"
Benazir: Emily is another of my lovers.
Paxman: You're quite a Mata Hari, aren't you?
Benazir: My friends sometimes call me Mata Bhutto. It's one of the things you learn in the Oxford Union.
Esler: I'm cut to the quick. You've two-timed me with Jeremy, three-timed me with Emily.
Benazir: How else was I to get a party political broadcast out of Newsnight?

─────

London scoffers fill London coffers.

─────

There was a beautiful moment of intrigued happiness in Jade's eyes.

─────

Brodie threw her curls around Alex like a lasso.

─────

Heliotrope & Hansie

"Where should we be without our stays?
Lost in a magical mountain maze,
Fished by St. Valentine from the gaze
Of men who would have us lose our stays."
They crossed a brook that was not Lethe
Yet changed their life like a bride's peethi
Elvi. The faun in Joan Lindsay's head,
Heat haze personified, brought Mount
Etna to Hanging Rock. She wrote at the cusp
Of the 'sixties about the cusp of the century,
Sensing perhaps change more than the normal
Change, looking back to look forward.
She plays with an outbreak of Ancient Greece,
Yet seen through Rome, showing England,
Seen through Melbourne, 1900,
Seen through 1959, Joan's adolescence
Recollected, layers on layers,
Like Victorian Victorian clothes,
Loose, when they cast off their stays
And all in a haze of imagination.
And Joan's time? Did writing take her out
Of her time yet deeper in to her time,
Giving her greater understanding?
What if a girl from Hanging Rock
Were on a beach in a bikini,
Not knowing how she got there,
Yet still with the sensibility of her time,
Not knowing the ways of these winding bays
Where none has ever been constricted
Or known the joy of taking off stays?

Is Didley Squat near Dingley Dell?
That is a secret for Mark Laurenson to tell.

Le Tombeau De Miles

Dribbling to Didley, crossing to Didley—
Austere as the public face of Nicholas Ridley
Is the commentator's lot when West Ham
And Manchester City are going at it, not hammer
And tongs, but biblical lion and lamb.
"A rum cup-tie, this." 'Too right—it's a bummer."
The fingers are numb and the mind's getting number.

―――――

Rafa isn't raffish; some would account him a dish.
He keeps the football faith alive like a Christian drawing a fish.

―――――

"He has chameleon D. N. A. . He can frame anyone for anything. No-one is safe."

   "How can it change at random?"

   "It replicates a sample—but, here's the cunning part: it can switch between two mimicked D. N. A.s, see-sawing malevolently so as to place two innocent people at the scene of a crime. It has even been murmured that it can imitate three."

   'Three. There's a powerful computer in that D. N. A.."

   "But it operates itself—we know that he and his D. N. A. are partners, we think the D. N. A. is the senior partner."

―――――

T. H. White thought of a megalomaniac on Rockall long before Fleming thought of one in the West Indies.

―――――

Preiti isn't British; Preiti is so pretty.
She has no London fetish, and Preiti is so witty.

She's pretty sound is Preiti, more than A 1 at Lloyd's.
Most of Gordon Brown's cabinet belong in Stanley Royd.
She's a bigger star than any in Gotham city.
Though she has a playback, she can even sing a ditty
Pleasingly, not through a haze of alcohol and cannabis
Like those who resemble Anubis, dog-headed London
Luminaries, cruel as Cheyenne dog soldiers
And cowardly.

—————

Put-down city, fake as Piltdown Man.
    "Would you characterise Gordon Brown as Piltdown Man in a kilt?"
    "Yes."

—————

"I prefer a 'Tush" to a "Pish'," said Philip. "It's discouraging when people keep pishing your copy. I've known sub-editors go on a pishing expedition, picking fault with every laboriously crafted sentence. It's enough to make you want to set the Jack Russells on them."

—————

Would a shape-shifter, such as Bjorn in 'The Hobbit', have different animals hovering at his shoulder, playing his soul in relays?

—————

How many people will be put off a handsome edition of 'The Jungle Books" by the editor's anonymous abuse of Kipling.

—————

Le Tombeau De Miles

According to Frank Tyson, teachers were paid four times as much in Australia as Great Britain in the late 'fifties. Did they have to go where they were sent?

―――――

"You take issue with cabals because they're men's cabals." (Harriet Harman)

―――――

The Dalai Lama was born in north-eastern Tibet. If the birthplaces of all the Dalai Lamas were marked, what would the pattern be? Would they make the shape of a bird or an animal? Dalai Lama means ocean of love, as in the song in "Seema". Tibetan cavalry rode white horses. Was it their armour which was inscribed with allusions to Allah? The Dalai Lama says "Peking" as I do. He remembers his father's vanity about his moustache. As soon as India became independent, the British mission was withdrawn from Lhasa.

―――――

Hoagy had the dreaded lurgy,
Felt much worse than Heidi's Ergi,
More like a diseased elm than an Alm-uncle.
What could Heidi do for Hoagy,
He who sang for Lauren and Bogey?
Heidi gathered Alpine herbs, mixed a potion,
Brewed it hot, was surprised at Hoagy's devotion
To it, for he had sneaked a snorter of whisky
In to a drink that should have made him frisky,
Ready for a ride in a jingling droshkey, but Hoagy slept
And Heidi had her suspicions.

―――――

Someone had said my mother's blueberry blue coat matched her eyes and she had treasured the compliment fifty years.

"My eyes were bluer then," she explained apologetically, regretting the wear and tear. In truth, they were still quite a deep blue, bright when happy.

―――――

Jade approached the car in a ballerina's drunken walk, legs crossing, then leaned on the bonnet. ("acting from the neck up"?)

―――――

"Boris Godunov" and Boris not good enough.
"I'm the most operatic mayor you'll get."

―――――

"My ancestor was a minister of the Sublime Porte. I'm in charge of the Great Wen.
 "Is there a Boris minor'?"
 'There's nothing minor about us, we tend to youthful spread, then middle-aged spread is the icing on the cake, proving how solid we are."
 "You're built like Peter Ustinov."

―――――

"When will London cease to be the Great Wen? That is the great when."
 "Did Boris ask you to write speeches for him?"
 'They come easily.'
 A blend of Peter Ustinov and Ronald Reagan but blond.
 "Steady on. I've never played Nero and I don't tell anecdotes of Hollywood."

―――――

Le Tombeau De Miles

Boris Johnson reminds me of Pyotr Stepanovich in Dostoevsky's 'The Possessed", who plays the buffoon yet is leader of a revolutionary cell.

Vanilla will do for me
When it's Dowland, white
As snow yet exotic with the conquests
Of Cortez, clear yet spiced.
(A hostile critic likened Emma Kirkby's voice to vanilla.)

Jeremy's no Jeremiah,
Saying Gordon's a pariah.
Jeremy lets the viewer decide;
He's the bulwark before the truth.
He even gives an economist ruth
In mellow mood. At other times, wrath
Falls deservedly on those who wriggle,
Who niggle the nation with their falsehoods.

Dancing as a marionette, Rani Mukherji was still able to dance freely, jerkily on strings but with an infinitesimal rubato conferring grace.
   "I'm in time. I just extend my movements slightly."
   The spirit wore purple for the shepherd's test. Onlookers thought the shepherd had tricked him but the spirit was willing. No stopper could stand between his love and his beloved.

"You name an elephant after me and call that a compliment!"

—————

Did my mother identify with the girl from Lark Rise, destined for better things?

—————

Roy came across Aznavour as he browsed on the radio. Bernd tilted his head back, savouring the song. Roy turned the dial. Bernd's head slowly came forward. He did not speak. He was back in Leeds.

—————

Jazzy he may be at times, but Aznavour sees blue with European connotations: blue is the opposite of grey skies; it is the blue flower of Novalis. Why not Armenian connotations? Would Jeremy Paxman like to referee a set-to between Aznavour and Professor Norman Stone about the Armenian massacres?

—————

Florence had knocked an elephant over and a tusk had come off. Playing with the tusk, she touched a secret spring under the elephant which only responded to the precise chemical composition of the tusk, and a door fell open. She peered inside and, as she held it up to her eyes, it got bigger and bigger and she got smaller and smaller until she was inside it as if she were a Greek hiding in the wooden horse outside Troy. What would the elephant do next? She had a look at the door to see how it slotted in and how she would get it open again after closing it. Then they were off. The elephant did a quick circuit of the living room to get its bearings, went in to the kitchen, then, with its trunk, unlocked the door. Ponies were passing. It soon caught up with them.

Florence would not have known a full-sized elephant if she had seen one but this was big. She peeped out through an aperture on the left, which could be closed like a knight's vizor, and found she was looking down on a pony's head. It whinnied. Florence tried to see the rider—a girl—who looked annoyed at being passed by an elephant and was urging her steed to race. But then the elephant used its bottom like a centre forward, nosed ahead, and beat the ponies to the bridge before Risley. It would not have seen off Sea The Stars but it was nifty. Then it turned for home, pausing to help itself to some fruit and flowers at the farm shop, pick up a hose and give itself a drenching, then it rang the bell and cunningly shrank. And while Florence's granny was looking to see who the visitor was, it sneaked in, the secret door opened, Florence fell out and was full-size by the time she landed on her feet.

Florence had a taste for adventure now. If you had been for a ride in an elephant, it would have whetted your appetite. She kept feeling the other ornaments to see if they had a secret door but without luck. Even the other elephants seemed to be normal. Granny had only one magical ornament. It was remiss of Granny.

─────

"I had a funny little granny," said my mother. "She used to make up stories about the neighbours. She had a pension she called her Lloyd George. She used to buy flowers and my mother would say: "Why don't you buy something we need?"

─────

Blatter falls like Blätter;
We'll shake off the fetters;
And to hell with Platini.
Onward, onward, scrap the offside law;
We'll storm E. U. A. F. A.,
Singing the old saw:

Blatter falls like Blätter;
We'll shake off the fetters;
And to hell with Platini.
Onward, onward, cast the blighters out;
Blighty stands, an impregnable redoubt.
Blatter...
Onward, onward, the sap is not in Sepp.
You can tell by his pronouncements that Sepp, he is a sap.

(to the famous tune from 'The Vagabond King")

─────

"Does Byron loom large in your life?"

"He did while I was working on "Arcadia". I felt I was beginning to write Byron, which is a pleasant change from being Rosencrantz and Guildenstern with nothing to say. Felicity said people could no longer mistake me for a Dick or Harry. Nor could they call it tommy-rot. This is pure Stoppard, using Byron as cheesecloth. There's usually a grain of truth in what Felicity says."

"Is "Indian Ink" a divertissement or something substantial in your canon?"

"It's in my canon. Martin Amis is so up-to-date he doesn't have a canon but a Kalashnikov. "Indian Ink" is like falling asleep to the sound of India and dreaming.

It's me at my most dreamy. That's why Felicity takes her bath-robe off."

─────

Did Palmerston walk in Fryston Wood, where I walked?

─────

Gandhi is only against caste when he is ostentatiously against caste.

–––––

What might she have done with Shakespeare's words who moved with paraphrase? Ablaze she spoke yet softly. (Jade)

–––––

A bright seventeen-year-old, who had enjoyed Jane Austen at fifteen, was assumed to be unable to understand Shakespeare. My mother read three Shakespeare plays by the age of fourteen and learned half a dozen speeches by heart. The only person I recall who had read all Dickens' novels was a school caretaker and former bricklayer, who had left school at fourteen. They should stop talking down to people on television. Brian Sewell said:
'Treat people as equals and they'll equal you."

–––––

An unreadable "Times" leader mentioned "Dickensian" language. Could we have some in "Times" leaders please?

–––––

Richie Benaud must be thankful not to live in Seven Network Sydney. He can sip chardonnay in the A. B. C. and go for a stroll in to Channel Nine without fear of crazy stalkers, psychotic junkies or deranged scriptwriters.

–––––

Mediaeval monarchs died of a surfeit but not of crazy stalkers.

–––––

"Jacques Brel is Flemish," said the Flemish fitter, "but his own people don't listen to him because he sings in French." He had nothing against Germans because of the Second World War but resented Walloon dominance of Belgium and was glad to see coal running out in Wallonia while Flanders still had large coal deposits and its industry was healthier. (How partial was his description?)

―――――

M. Balladur attended a simple ceremony at Les Invalides.
M. Balladur: Frenchmen and women, it is with a heavy heart that I lay down my subjunctives for my country. They have kept me company through good years and bad, through a long and contented marriage, through service in modest roles, less modest roles, almost the greatest office. They have fitted my tongue like a glove. Now France has called on me to make a sacrifice and I am ready. I lay down this wreath. The symbiosis of my soul and my subjunctives is at an end. (wipes away a tear).

―――――

Brown, light blue, greenish grey. Both parents have blue eyes.
Surely, Kirsty is the odd one out.
(making the reader think.)

―――――

Anjana's spread among the stars, knowing where they are,
Knowing, unlike Shelley, all about the rainbow.
She has space within her, she knows
Between her whizzing atoms.

―――――

Le Tombeau De Miles

Susan's father called her Bunty. Did she enjoy confiding that to boys, letting us in to the secret of her father's affection?

Does a person's favourite colour vary according to the light in which he or she grows up?

"It's said that Jane Austen went secretly in to the harem in Istanbul to smooth over relations between a captured Frenchwoman and the Sultan, who eventually took her to wife. Palmerston, who was Secretary at War, paid tribute to her diplomatic skills in a secret memorandum, which has lately come to light. The Sultan would have liked her to stay, teaching etiquette and social graces to his wives and concubines, but she regretted she could not accept, having a novel to finish. Jane Austen might have re-written the Eastern Question."

"Riesling goes to your heart, not your head."

"It's well-known," said Miles, 'that two of Jane Austen's brothers were in the Navy. Wishing to extend her experience, she disguised herself as, first one, then the other for a voyage to the West Indies and a tour of duty in the Mediterranean; hence Jane's Fighting Ships."

Jane Austen's father, related to Warren Hastings, Governor-general of Bengal, took a commission for arranging the sale of goods sent back by Hastings. Did Jane handle Indian jewellery and materials she could not possibly afford to buy? She loved the sea. Would she have made the Grand Tour, given the chance, or married an East India Company administrator? Did she instinctively cling to England because that was where her readership was?

    She left her inspiration behind in Hampshire when the family moved to Bath.

―――――

From sentenced-to-death Tom Dooley
To renowned, rich Anthony Rooley
There are many kinds of music
But few are ubiquitous musak
With none of the grace of the Cossack
But brutal as his whip. No Attic
Sophistication here; Asda's belting it out.
We all know its buying power has clout;
So do its speakers; raucous, arrhythmic,
They flout the rules of salesmanship. (I hope he is rich.)

―――――

Maleficent Millicent did for "Frasier".

―――――

They rhyme Sharapova with Saratoga.
Have they stealth bombed the language too?
Karenina, Gordeeva, Moiseyeva, Morozova:
I feel morose when melody is rejected.
Those with an ear must feel dejected.
Venevitinova, Vedeneeva: names to savour.

―――――

A woman killed in Pompeii had one yellow, skeletal hand, one chocolate, yet the yellow hand was said to be the one with which she had tried to shield her face. Pliny the Younger's account has been vindicated by observation of recent eruptions. A pyroclastic explosion is what gave the inhabitants of Pompeii and Herculaneum no chance to flee.

"L'Atalantide"
The skipper's wife wore a polka-dot dressing-gown. When he tossed and turned in bed, thinking of her, dots were superimposed on the picture; she lay in another bed, somewhere in Paris, dots superimposed, recalling the garment she had worn in the bridal chamber. "L'Atalantide" had a grim beauty, evoking the cold and dampness of winter on the river, the cramped quarters aboard a barge, the difficulty in keeping things clean, but also the exhilaration of a fresh breeze, transfiguring shafts of sunlight, the joy of rising untrammelled. The couple were poor enough to delight in a song or a scarf; they delighted, too, in the depth of their own feelings.

Prévert, if it was Prévert, was a jongleur playing with words as he did card tricks or fooled with a woman's heart. He was proud of his backward cartwheel, repeated to the applause of tavern-goers, and would similarly have used his songs to topple back in to her arms, given half a chance. Love, cards, acrobatics—it was all evidently much the same to him.

"Skipper's mate" warmed to the very man who had cheated her of an evening on the town, the crusty mate; and he had been pleased to show her his curios and his tattoos—even the pickled hands that were all that remained of a friend. The macabre and the homely came together as she wrapped her skirt around the old sea-dog, complimented him on his "girl's waist" and set to pinning it in to the right shape for herself. Her new husband flew in to a passion at this familiarity, not wanting his bride contaminated by the coarseness of his shipmates.

A mythological name for a barge that plies between Paris and ports up and down the Seine was in keeping with Vigo's poetic conception of apparently humdrum lives—which he showed glittering with passion, frustrated dreams, hopes which soared from the cockpit like a navigator's gaze at the stars, even though that navigator was confined between two banks. "bavant boue et rubis" is Mallarmé's description of Baudelaire's poetry. Vigo evoked mud, fog, the most banal of cargoes, a cat having kittens in the marital bed, but also the romance of Parisian lights, seen from a barge moving in from the provinces, and of a tender heart, without fenders. His very first film had begun with steam billowing past a train window and music beating mechanically towards its destination. Did he see human life as looking out from an illuminated barge or train compartment in to darkness and being borne along rails or river to an unknown destination?

Incongruous and proud, the skipper's wife walked in her wedding-dress through the village to the landing-stage where the barge was moored. There was apparently no money for a reception but she would wash on her wedding day if need be to establish credentials to respectability. Her claim that he would see his true love under water drove him to dive in to the river and stay under as long as possible, searching for confirmation that she was his appointed mate. Indeed, he saw her—more clearly perhaps than he had seen aught else since she had gone away and he had left Paris, mortified. He had done business in a dream. Only when the embodiment of his dream returned could he do his work properly. Nearly sacked, he had been saved by his mate's loyalty. Which was Vigo most like: skipper, wife, drowsy mate? He was young to be as travelled as the mate. Vigo plays on the ambiguity of "mate", pointing the intensity of the relationship of captain and long-serving mate. Did Maurice Jarre compose the original music, so evocative of mist on the river, clammy dawns, struggling love?

Le Tombeau De Miles

Sewell ducked the challenge of explaining why Cézanne is great, not even mentioning which pictures he particularly liked and which, if any, left him cold. He did pour cold water on the idea that Cézanne is the father of every modernism.

Zola's painter based on Cézanne needed the stimulus of Paris and his friends; Cézanne did not.

"If they're going to make it far-fetched, why don't they have fun? The Grand Duchess Anastasia was such a fine actress she became Alf Stewart's grandmother without anyone suspecting she was Russian. Alf is heir to All the Russias."

Indians distinguish between root vegetables and others. Who decided that potatoes are weakening? Whole milk gives strength; cheese takes it away; red meat does.

Why should Wordsworth's legs appear bone-white to a young Frenchwoman in Paris? Her legs would not be exposed to the sun and his, being hairy, would very likely be darker. She was a royalist, Annette Vallon—she bore him a daughter. Prescient, she called him "Mr. Williams".

The Indian woman persisted in the pronunciation of Kenya she had learned in childhood, however much Kamlesh assailed her with his short vowel. He had left Nairobi as a baby. Was that why he aligned himself with Matthew Parris or was there a hidden agenda?

A spark seemed to fly from the hot tap towards the shower-tray, then I realised that the sun had come out and a bird had flown across it.

The best British generals have usually come from the same class as the incompetents, in particular, the country gentry.

On the landing, there was a smell of damp shower curtains, damp newspapers at the foot of the stairs, lavender and beeswax polish, and dianthus. Which wine would Jane McQuitty have recognised?

Is Sydney as exciting to a boy from the bush as Europe to someone from Sydney?

In 1932-33, Bradman's striking rate was 77 per hundred balls, about the same as Gilchrist's.

"He's a big noise at the B. B. C.. Keep it quiet."

Was there for Calista a brighter vista before the press tried to din in to her that she is skinny?

─────

Does anyone decorate the house with pictures of goldfinches for Diwali as robins appear on Christmas cards?

─────

Cruickshank found ramshackle houses spick and span inside. Only in the nineteen seventies had the state government provided any sanitation but the inhabitants took pride in making their slum something other than a slum. "Rama looks after the ramshackle". Some of the houses must have been rather like Daniel Peggoty's house at Yarmouth. Children in the Bombay slum did not look at the camera with hatred as in some Indian cities.

In the mosque at Damascus, people prayed, unconcerned by the cameras and the presence of an infidel. A Christian family have lived in Damascus for generations in harmony with their neighbours. There is even a Jewish quarter. Little remained of a mosaic but the picture of paradise was beautiful.

─────

George Osborne is in good company. Napoleon was betrayed by a Rothschild after giving Jews civil rights in the Papal States and Poland (as his brother, Jérome did in Westphalia).

─────

George Osborne said he thinks about the economy every second of the day. Greg Chappell wrote that a batsman needs to relax between overs.

─────

Bernd was round-faced. Did he feel that a round room chimed with his round face? He had a round room at home in Konstanz but, presumably, not at university. Was his an all-round mind, doing maths problems for fun besides having a passion for literature? I observed that he liked quiet music (a Bécaud song he described as "heavy"). John said he danced around to some jazz. Did Bernd ever become a roulette croupier? He thought it would give him time for writing and study. That winter, he wore a sheepskin bolero, not a waistcoat, as I learned when my mother wore one, probably not so thick—I remember his looked luxuriously warm. The other person with whom I associate the garment is the Czech girl who played Cinderella and had one of the prettiest faces I've seen, prettier than Audrey Hepburn. Left over from happier times, it lent a rustic opulence to her appearance as though she were an aristocrat "slumming it" in the Forest of Arden. I had thought her brunette; in colour, she was red-haired. The prince wore a scarlet hat, red answering her red, different shades, hers deeper, his, as yet, mere clothing, but soon she would blush the life through him, strum him like a lute. He knew not what sweet perils lurked in the forest. The colour of her eyes was less noticeable than the flutter of her lashes and the modelling of her face.

"You'll ride to your first ball like a hussar," her father had said. Her mother had promised her a dress pink as summer dawn but it was a blue dress which unfurled when a hazel nut cracked. The prince had a wide gold collar on his tunic, reminiscent of cavalier dress, though the period style was of mid-fifteenth century Burgundy. She sang a wordless song as she washed clothes at a brook amid the snow. She shot a bird of prey, otherwise was a friend of all animals, taking counsel from an owl

─────

"I suppose Bernd will become a professor," I suggested to our landlady.

"He says it's not like here. You have to know the right people."

So he thought there was appointment on merit in England yet

he was scornful of Leeds English department, asking why students put up with the lectures.

─────

"I like the way this young man attacks the weights," observed Roy. He had the calm perseverance of a leg-spinner who once dismissed Boycott in a house match (after taking some punishment) and a jazz fan who used to pick out Thelonious Monk's "Round Midnight" on the piano. He relished a physical challenge but had given up playing rugby after his collarbone was broken a second time, instead doing weight-training partly to build up muscles around the vulnerable bone. On seeing me, the deputy head declared:

"He doesn't lift weights by strength; he does it with nervous energy."

─────

A reflection of the moon floated below in a marriage of light, uneasily poised against the clouds while, stark and bright, a motel challenged the surrounding hills with its crest of lights which put me in mind of an airfield control tower. Lights were steady on the low ground close to Darley Dale yet they twinkled up the hills like stars as though they were closer to nature there and took on its properties. Shadowy horses roamed in a meadow beside the road, so deep in gloom that I thought for a moment they were cows. Many feet below, a brook dashed past, toothed with stones. Stone was the keynote in all this region: stone-built houses, dry stone walls, yet trees abounded here, softening the sky-line and in autumn enriching all.

It was the time of year for sunsets and westward was the way to walk in the early evening, drawn on by the sun. The higher glens still lay in a day of their own while the land below reached in to night.

─────

Susan was the mirror of his soul, cloister-quiet but humming with ideas. Her face, upturned, had bones that he gloated over, like a delicate porcelain cup. Her hair embodied sunshine. The rest of her was a flowing and a grace. He no more knew the parts than the individual blooms of a flower-bed.

Her hair was strewn with grass, green highlights just a shade from the shadow of her eyes.

―――――

Tanya Feifer's clothes expressed intelligence yet were carefully chosen to avoid giving the impression of a bluestocking.

―――――

When asked to compare himself with Brassens, Brel said:
"People of the north are more mystical."
How does that work in the southern hemisphere? Is David Boon more mystical than people in Brisbane?

―――――

"I only had to go to school in clogs once. There was a stuck-up blonde girl, who had said: "You must come round to our house." When she saw the clogs, she said: "It'll have to be another time." She never asked me again."

―――――

"My mother darned white cotton lisle stockings with black cotton. I put my foot down and refused to go to school in them. They were surprised because I usually accepted things but I would not go to school with stockings darned black."

―――――

Le Tombeau De Miles

I'd like one of Josephine's roses—or one descended from them—a whiff of Malmaison.

"I smell her!" exclaimed Bernd. "I like to smell women," he added with gusto.

"What a man!" exclaimed my mother of the plumber in "Neighbours", enjoying his impossibility.

This son of the manse knows less about business than the merchants of the Hanse.
 "Danse, danse with the Hanse," cried Jonathan Meades. 'These Lubeck buildings raise my spirits. They put me in Trenet mood. He's not the tops but he spreads joie de vivre. Waldemar Janusczak could do with him more than I, not being in equilibrium in his humours."

Jonathan Meades prefers Leeds Town Hall to the Alhambra.
"I wish I could swap my years in Leeds for yours in France."

Why Alastair Campbell on Jacques Brel? He claims to have listened to Brel more than any other musician in the past thirty years but does not ring true. He has just been pleased to discover that Brel was left wing; I heard him describe himself as "Left without shading" long ago; he also said he had a great weakness for Mendès-France, who was liberal rather than socialist. Meades is a connoisseur of Brel and writes perceptively about him.

―――――

How much of a romantic is Jonathan Meades? How much does he think he is?

―――――

"I like to mock a man wearing a funny hat," said Jacques Brel, "but I also like to lie in a meadow at four o'clock in the morning, watching the clouds pass."

―――――

Brel said one of his ambitions was to sail around the Mediterranean, calling at small ports off the beaten track. Was he only able to sail part of the way before leaving for the Pacific?

―――――

Clara and Robert were together at last.
"Who's gonna shoe your pretty little feet?"
Schumann.

―――――

Mrs Hewitt looked jubilant, her face clouded momentarily as she became aware of the cameras, then she determined to be happy and show she was happy

―――――

Le Tombeau De Miles

"I'm at Bec's beck and call, except when I'm on court, when I'm at the mercy of the linesman's call."

—————

"bec de plume," wrote Mallarmé. Is Bec a Bec de plume, one who inspires poets or a trying out of a pen, an aspiring work of art in herself? She eschews the -y, so ubiquitous in the columns of 'Times' women. "Home and Away" writers have been fond of girls' names ending in -y (not so much now). They've turned over a new leaf in the book of names.

—————

"Five and twenty, Wayne Rooney," calmed the referee. "Five and twenty."

—————

Is Gallas more Callas than Pallas Athene?
"We'd take on the world if we had Athene
Whispering encouragement in our ears,
Spreading her fragrance in a world of liniment.
We'd foil Wayne Rooney as easy as a Cyclops,
Resist Ronaldo more easily than Sirens.
We'd stand firm in the environs
Of Stoke, repel long throws, then go for broke.
We may be foreign but we've hearts of oak.
Our fame would extend from the Soke
Of Peterborough to Roanoke.

—————

I heard Phil in Leeds when Don was ill,
The supporting acts rubbish but not over-amplified

Heliotrope & Hansie

As when Bernd and John went to hear Duke Ellington
Two and a half years later—that marks a turning-point.
My landlady was there, unknown to me then,
And thought him too serious, clad in black,
Not fun like the Beatles. A student I met on a train
Agreed with me: "A very polished performance."
Now I could hear their harmony for the first time
But when they were many years past their prime.
It would be like hearing Sinatra live in the late 'eighties.
Cool or hot,
Those melodies which intertwine as in a kissing-knot
Were as much part of my adolescence
As the thrilling dissonance, complement
To Shostakovich, one of whose themes
Was likened to a Young Pioneer tune.
They too were pioneers, of harmony,
Influencing the Beatles. The London media
Pretended not to notice: they were 'fifties;
Now it was 'sixties. But, at least, they had
A decade—or part of a decade.
I might have grown up
With Shankar and Jaikishen but I grew up
With the Everly Brothers.

Chapter Eight

Punter

Cool head out of Corsica, able to steer without Baedeker,
Knowing the scent of his island from out at sea,
Restoring a France that was all at sea,
Outdoing the wanderer from Ithaca,
He put an end to the Terror, long cheered on
By Thomas Jefferson, and he kept no slaves.
He sought honour, not to hack the heads of aristos'
Chamber-maids and call it the will of the people.
Witnessing the massacre at the Tuileries,
He saved the life of a Swiss Guard.
In Russia, he said: 'There are no enemies
After a battle; only men."
Inured to blood, able to take it in his stride,
He took no pride in it, sought to end discord,
Preferring the Media Via to Hemingway.
His Concordat gave the faithful back their Sunday.
He found treasure in Egypt long before Tutankhamun.
Mathematician, he measured the Pyramids
In terms of France, the country he had chosen
To serve (no-one knows whether he applied
To join the Royal Navy and was ignored.)
He found an empty treasury and left it full,
Balancing budgets, not borrowing to impoverish
Future generations. Worthless paper gave way
To trusted coins: the gold napoleon is a far cry

From Royal Bank of Scotland finance.
Soldiers had not been paid, fed or clothed;
Civil servants were months behind with their salary;
Foundlings had died for lack of money.
France was under attack on so many frontiers.
He had more nous than a son of the manse,
More modesty than a Mountbatten.
His New Deal was real, not propaganda.
Despite Pitt's plots, he kept the ideals of the Revolution
Alive for fifteen years and proved they could produce
Order and a civilised society. Ever-resourceful,
He made the Pyramids a means of raising morale.
Looters he shamed by mockery, not the British
Army's flogging. His directives were not distraction
From inaction. He did something,
Such as putting a lightning-conductor on St. Peter's, Rome.
Botanists he took on campaign to seek rare flowers for Josephine
As he took scientists to Egypt.
(Her roses were given a safe-conduct through the British blockade.)
Born on an island, thwarted by an island,
He ended his days on an island.
Josephine came to him across the Atlantic.
When he sailed the Atlantic,
He was on his way to captivity.

—————

"King Creole" may be lively but the Creole empress won more hearts.

—————

Elba was only put on the map by Napoleon. "All power to your Elba."

—————

Punter

Kenneth Cranham had energy and sullenness but not the idealism
and nobility of countenance. (playing Napoleon)

—————

Paolette ran up a path to scrump an apple. Her tête a tête with
Fréron is more exciting than anything in Harry Potter.

—————

Paoletta was frivolous, they say,
Yet obdurate as Peter May
When rebels besieged Port-au-prince.
She had her chair taken outside to raise
Morale. Unable to hold a lance,
She had the spirit of a lancer
Or Gérard's hussars of Conflans.
She stuck her tongue out at Josephine
And never quite became a queen
Herself. The two were too easygoing
Not to become friends in time.
She had no fear of posing for Canova
(The room once warmed) but would
Have been no sport of Casanova.
Open-hearted, she sent her chef to St. Helena
To brighten her brother's exile.
By then he could eat little.

—————

Spotting walking through Notting Hill
Hugh and Julia, hiding from the hue
And cry of photographers, seeking
A yuletide tryst, I looked around
For covert filming a la "Bowfinger".

There was no dead ringer for Hugh.
"Would you like to stay the night?"
"I'd like to stay the night's course for ever."
"You'll have to cross the landlady's palm with silver."
'To hell with money. This is a night of lust."
"I hope you are insatiable as an elephant in musth."
"A red mist of musth oft comes before my eyes
But I calm down with all your satisfied sighs
And lie in dreamland till the sun arise."
(archaic language for an archaic character—or is it just that Richard Curtis' jokes are old?)

─────

Is there invisible ink in "Indian Ink", ideas which are only noticed by the cognoscenti or after a decent interval which testifies to their subtlety? If Felicity Kendall had to jump forward and back from scene to scene, that would be a recipe for comic chaos.

Beethoven read Hindu scriptures circa 1810-20. 'There's food for Stoppard." Was Beethoven trying to turn himself in to a mystic by means of his own music? Did Beethoven ever read descriptions of ragas? (unlikely)

Stoppard cast about for a subject.

"I feel like metempsychosis," he told Felicity. "You be me and write a play. I'll be you and do a spot of acting."

"You'll be me over my dead body."

─────

Stoppard's Indian erudition failed to impress an Indian, not altogether helped by Art Malik's enunciation. How fine is Felicity's mosquito net?

"Stoppard intellectual? I'd never thought of that."

Tungku is familiar with Billy Bunter. Did he read him at school? Does Stoppard always show his knowledge in such a way as to put people's backs up? "What does he know? Does he only appear to know?" After Nightingale's benediction, a less approving review, not a bad night out, but shallow.

"Poor Tom's not a-cold but out in the cold. He tried to swallow India whole—as far as he could in a crash course—be the Kipling of the millennium—and he came a cropper, no, he under-achieved. His vintage cars were fun but they weren't high-powered. Felicity was fun but she wasn't high-powered. It's not Art Malik's destiny to be fun. Has Stoppard applied his antennae to Bengal, to Bombay, Madras, Delhi, village India, ancient India, whizz-kid India? He seems to want us to think him all-embracing."

———

As I closed the cupboard, there was a sound like Ennio Morricone's music for "A Fistful of Dollars", not quite the orchestral whinny at the end of "Bruxelles".

———

"What if your favourite language doesn't match your favourite people? Where would you choose to live?"

———

Keats had never been so exciting and beautiful as the titles of Françoise Hardy songs I read on the record covers. They were the gateway to a new world. Most of them were as yet mysterious; I had heard the imaginative French arrangements, discreet behind the clear, beautiful voice that was not afraid to draw attention to itself. Her voice was darker on the second L. P., already more knocked about by fortune and the demands of touring but hungry for life.

———

Rainer observed that Françoise Hardy sang without vibrato, then that she did in "Pars", which I later heard her say she particularly liked.

―――――

Bernd told John he liked darkness in front of his eyes. John, who was full of affectation, thought this affected. Did Bernd want to observe without being observed? He wore sun-glasses when out for the day with John, so was it John he wanted to observe?

―――――

Rainer, singing in his bath, was disconcerted to hear the sound of laughter outside. Bernd was a singer too but not in the bath.

―――――

"Is my O right?" asked Rainer.
　"Would you repeat it?" He did so. I considered it for a moment.
　"I think that's all right."
　If I got in too deep here, I should begin to doubt my own O.

―――――

Mr. AlIton was wont to describe himself as a rose between two thorns. Gillian Tett might have been so described, sitting between two bankers or ex-chancellors. One day, in the music hut, I smoothed down my pullover self-consciously. Mr. AlIton mockingly imitated me for the amusement of the class.

―――――

I arrived back from the university before most of the others. Bernd was waiting in the big room assigned for our study; he had heard me enter the house and as soon as I opened the door, first checking that I was alone, he opened the door of a sideboard and took out a book.

"I saw that Rainer had this book yesterday; I have [t at home. "Apparition" is in it. We must be quick, before Rainer comes in."

He opened the book at the right page, put it on the table and invited me to read 'the most beautiful poem" he knew, which "takes anyone of sensibility in to a world of faerie". I liked it.

'The beginning and the end are particularly fine," he observed. When I had written out, without telling him what they were, the first four lines of Shakespeare's Sonnet 73, he had commented that they were "comfortable" and that all the words were cold except yellow but that was stronger than the rest. Mallarmé's opening phrase, "La lune s'attristait was immediately atmospheric but I had mixed feelings about the seraphim, written so perfectly for sound and look on the page but, as so often in early Mallarmé, inclined to préciosité; the end was faultless and I liked the middle. Some weeks later I bought Mallarmé's poems (exquisitely printed) and found "Sainte" and "Autre Eventail" perfect examples of Mallarmean poetry, beyond préciosité, expressing so much indirectly. "Paint, not the thing, but the effect it produces," he wrote. Imagination in his readers helps. A few years later, I was to say that, when reading 'the extreme west of desire", you should be thinking of John Cabot sailing out from Bristol to explore the coast of Canada.

Actors and directors often say that Shakespeare wrote for the stage, not the page. Oddly, there are passages in 'The Winter's Tale", 'Twelfth Night" and "Antony and Cleopatra" (and others), which have a beauty of texture and colour on the page beyond almost any other English writer. Shakespeare did not mind his plays being read; and theatrical people have been surprised to discover that Elizabethan and Jacobean theatres were smaller than had been supposed, the acting style therefore more intimate, closer to Cary Grant than Olivier.

―――――

Shakespeare without the poetry is like the St. Matthew Passion without the music.

─ ─ ─ ─ ─

"Everyone's television is glaring, except ours," said my mother. In that respect at least, she was one up on the world.

"I've never liked variety." Having curiosity, she preferred films. It was a treat for her when she had the chance to see films on television; it made up for so much else. Amsterdam disappointed her after keeping it in her memory for nearly fifty years. Drug addicts congregating in the city centre and prostitutes sitting in shop windows were a far cry from the old Amsterdam she had savoured. She had always liked the sound of New Zealand, might have gone there, had fate been different.

─ ─ ─ ─ ─

I never knew my mother had mother-of-pearl. (W. C. Fields' imprecation). I remembered a tortoiseshell lid on a container on her dressing-table. Mother-of-pearl, tortoiseshell—was she attracted by their names as well as their look, as I was?

─ ─ ─ ─ ─

"Hutchinson was running you down," said Susan. "He needn't think we don't like you." I had already heard that he had told the Lower Sixth he thought I was conceited.

─ ─ ─ ─ ─

"Don't be afraid to tell people you can do the job," advised my father. (not much point if they call you conceited.)

─ ─ ─ ─ ─

'The only time I've been in Australia, I was locked up. It was at the oil terminal near Fremantle. There was a bit of trouble in a bar and I spent a night in the cells."

Did Vic pore over maps of Australia, looking for the places he had known? Had he hoped to settle there? Did he ever have dreams of going back?

"I said that I'd translate this book and I'm leaving tomorrow," said Bernd. "We'd better start on the bus."
 As soon as we sat down, he opened his book on modern lyric poetry.
 "Rimbaud wrote: we should not say: I think, but I am thunk—thought. Elevenpenny please." He was less aware of the incongruity than I was.

Fräulein Stinshof said of "Las de l'amer repos", 'This is music." She liked Rimbaud's "Ophélie" but thought "Les Assis" shallow.
 "Where there is melancholy, there is depth," she said of Heine. She also liked Verlaine. Which was her favourite Verlaine poem? I should have asked her. She thought no-one was wholly evil. There were pupils in that school who might have disillusioned her. She looked younger than she was, so I, at first, mistook her for a schoolgirl come from another school to take some G. C. S. E. exam. She wore a navy blue blazer and a white frock.

"Devi" is set in 1860. At the Hindu festival, "Colonel Bogey" is played, an incongruous reminder of the juxtaposition of religiosity and

Western modernity. It suited the Indian government to promote "Mother India", in which Nargis recounts the hardships of her life and welcomes the Nehru government's dam, which will relieve rural poverty. Satyajit Ray is critical of feudalism, the caste system, traditional Hindu practices, fragile film stardom, business ethics in Calcutta—he is not a comfortable film-maker for the political establishment. "The Company" is the most French of his films that I've seen: it describes the gradual corruption by compromise of a young graduate from the provinces who yearns for his lost idealism when his sister-in-law brings a reminder of it. Yet he continues to rise in the company by laying aside his scruples.

─────

Nitin Sawhney's music for "A Throw of Dice" has an Indian flavour yet is like Prokoviev at his most lyrical ("Romeo and Juliet", "Cinderella", the first violin concerto).

─────

Encountering Kane in the hospital corridor, Dani seemed to roll thoughts around her head and lips, her tone changing from syllable to syllable. Dani steeled herself to thank him.
(So Australian acting is the worst in the world, as nothing could be more boring than Belgian popular music. Three of the most talented composer/performers of the century were born in Belgium or grew up there.)

─────

"I'll invest in a cup of coffee," said Gordon Brown. "I'll expect my money back with ten per cent interest."

─────

Punter

"Gordon Brown is to be the new manager of Portsmouth Football Club. He may do better than Harry Redknapp, winning the Premiership and the Champions' League with players the club can't afford."

'That's my idea of economics," said Gordon Brown.

———

Rumour has it that Tony Blair and Peter Mandelson plotted against Gordon Brown when he had gone to invest a penny.

———

They all wore pointed silver paper hats. Jade's was not as bright as the others in the half-light. Had they given her a less shiny one because of her blonde hair or did she not have the silver tinsel around the base of the hat?

———

I have rolled away my life with wheelie bins,
Stumbled at the foot of the stairs, turning sharply,
Cardboard underfoot, liable to sprain my ankle—
What a joy is recycling, especially for those in flats,
Who have even less room to swing a cat
At council workers, who look gone-out at carefully sorted bags
And leave them, who arrive at the crack of dawn
In the hope that bins will not have been put out
To save themselves work. Let us abase ourselves
Before the wheelie bin as before Jagganath.

———

The yellow shirt does not go pale by electric light so much as by half-light, just as the yellow kalanchöe was white when the kitchen light was on but not that at the top of the stairs. Yellow pales on the fringe of the pool of light.

―――――

An X-ray showed that Poussin had not altered the painting.
 "Damn," said Henry Lincoln. I liked his sense of humour. It was a "damn" with a comma, not an exclamation mark.

―――――

Paxman made a show of questioning aggressively, knowing that Heseltine could refute his arguments. It reminded me of Keith Miller bowling an eight ball over of bouncers to Arthur Morris in a benefit match. They were all dispatched to the boundary. Paxman was like a lawyer arguing a brief.

―――――

Paxman enjoyed saying deliquescence, asserting a rich vocabulary in a barbaric time.

―――――

Picasso's "picture in a box" had interesting shapes and colours. The other five, by Matisse, Pollock, Rothko and others, were empty, devoid of interest and meaning. The French garden and street scenes were pretty and painterly, though some people would have dismissed them as being like photographs.

―――――

Did Leonardo and Napoleon both have Etruscan blood?

―――――

Punter

Gloria threatened to divest me of my trousers.
  "I'm the one who'll be taking your trousers off," she warned as I left the canteen. Would it have made her Gloria in excelsis, had they caught me?

─────

Don't ask for help from Hilfenhaus.
Though he be as quiet as a mouse,
More dignified than Stanley Rous,
He's still a bowler, Hilfenhaus,
Keen to rap knuckles, tilt at helmets,
Bounce as high as the highest pelmets.
Be you from Leeds or the Vale of Elmete,
Beware that probing Hilfenhaus.

─────

I prefer Punter to Pinter.
I should think Pinter
Preferred Punter to Pinter,
Since a love of cricket was his saving grace.
Ve—ry slow, Pinter.
He never wrote a Gower of a script.
(Ricky Ponting's nickname)

─────

The Georgian age is finite;
The age of Georges is timeless;
He was never found to be rhymeless.
He scented his time with thyme, with lavender
And whichever other herbs abound in the maquis
Above Sète. He grew up between a lake
And the Mediterranean, the Pyrenees near at hand.
Villon was dear to his heart at school, as a schoolfellow

Remembered. A fifteenth century poem was played
On the radio, thanks to Georges; Paul Fort is known
To millions, thanks to Georges; and the author of "Les Philistins"
Would have delighted in the song's fame. Melodist
Of genius, Brassens is not just a setter of words;
He sets his own words, occasionally gross, far more
Often delicate, playfully in the ear, like a child
In a rock-pool, pearls and jellyfish, stones washed
Across the sea, across centuries, Penelope
Read about in Sete to inspire him long afterwards.
Conflict in the Catholic Church prompts Georges
To ruefully disarming humour, peacemaking
As far as he can. Stern "Sixty-eighters" are put in their place
With a reminder of the deaths that follow from fanaticism.
Philosophically an anarchist, he was peaceful.
(How can there be a society of anarchists?
He belonged to one just after the second world war.)
He made music a lightning conductor for dissent,
Prompting thought, not riots. His default setting
Was tenderness, laced with humour; whetting
His blade against injustice from time to time,
He made his banned gorilla famous.
"Je suis un ours, un solitaire."
But one full of humanity.
Invited to join the Académie Francaise, he declined,
Preferring his place in the wings.
"I thought I was a great poet and I was wrong."
Were you, Georges?

─────

"Guillaume," said Mr. Wright, "we must decide what to do about the jubilee." I probably looked supportive but not enthusiastic.

─────

"Is that one of your own?" asked my mother when I used the word, inwardness.

"No. It's German. Innigkeit."

─────

"Would you come in with me?" asked Susan. The company of the familiar, snubbed one made it easier to face the Parkinson Court.

─────

"You'll have to learn to fence with a moonbeam against lightning. A magic wand would be shrivelled up but cool moonlight can ride out heat. Some suspect that, if the Earth were destroyed by a conflagration, moonlight would nurse ft back to life, would be the nanny of all future things."

─────

I had an impression of a green pendant but her eyes would not let me look.

─────

"Greta remembered that I had a nice yellow coat." It was a fond memory for her. There are certain clothes which are just right or happen to coincide with happy times.

─────

"I've always wanted to live in a house with white walls." And so she did for the last sixteen years of her life. Had she taken a fancy to white walls when reading a book long ago?

─────

Heliotrope & Hansie

'The arrangements on your French records are more imaginative," said Roy, a Sinatra fan.
 "Brel?"
 "All of them."

─────

Henry's hand will forever haunt him;
Who had a hand in Henry's hand?
Diverse divers, cloggers, skivers, bloggers,
Convinced of their club's perfection.
Tyldesley's a brick in football's edifice,
Tyldesley, the voice of Lancashire clubs.
You should have been Mancunian, Thierry.

─────

There's no lethargy when Lataji sings;
There's no "Sloop John B." when Lataji sings;
No skirl or scat, no callow Take That;
You have to take off your hat
When Lataji sings.

─────

I first heard Jacques Brel singing "Mathilde", his voice riding like a Valkyrie over the orchestra.

─────

He dabbled in derivatives. Why so do Fry and Laurie.
Finance has changed since Adam Smith and Burns and "Annie
 Laurie".
But making money is the thing, the way to make the grade

Punter

And putting the frosting on the cake takes more than safe, small
    loans.
Tokyo's in a tulip-rage of speculation, hence peculation.
There'll be no baring of souls, no plugging of holes,
Only a shrugging of shoulders at their rivals, yet a corporate mugging
Could happen to anyone without sound business practice.

—————

Tchaikovsky's violin concerto was composed in Italy. Did it sound
Italian to a Russian, Russian to an Italian? And what to a German?

—————

Would Monk have monk on if he knew
That you preferred Miles Davis' "Round Midnight"
To his own? Their jam-jousts would have to be
In Heaven. "It was written for the piano,
So it's better on the piano." "Bach praised God
With trumpets; they're not ethereal but they're cool,
Not sensuous as the clarinet but sensuous enough
When I'm playing—and the brightness!"
"Blowing your own trumpet again. The piano talks back—
I'm not alone in saying that—a multiplicity of fingers
And keys communing with each other:
Play the piano alone and you're being gregarious."
But the melody they agreed on.

—————

Thelonious, not always euphonious,
Like Prokoviev
Deliberately discordant at times

—————

"George Eliot was a great person," said Susan. "She lived with a man—not like that."

―――――

Connors wore a light blue jacket with a green tie as though distantly harmonising with the officials' uniforms while keeping his individuality.

―――――

"I have a tryst with destiny," says Obama.
While middle America watches a film about a heist,
Obama takes soundings on the zeitgeist—
Does he not know by instinct?

―――――

Hong Kong's steamy bustle spread upwards, even unawares, as though it were fleeing communism, which came from the circles of hell.

―――――

Paxman had a tot of rum for Trafalgar. What will he drink for Austerlitz?

―――――

How many antique scarves has Isabelle? Does she remember where she bought each? Are they arranged by colour or country of origin? How does she feel when she handles something from Algeria, Turkey or Germany?
    "I hoped for a thousand and one nights with one man but I had to make do with fleeting loves—except for acting and my children."

Punter

"Is Ataturk your kind of Turk?"

"Not so far off, but I'm half-German, born in France, so no Turk is quite my kind of Turk. Had fate destined me for a harem, I should have missed so much."

─────

Diaby is known from Paris to Blaby.

─────

Napoleon's thoughts outran his pen. Was that before Pitt's agents began poisoning him? French scientists found arsenic in locks of his hair from 1805 and 1812 as well as from the years on St. Helena.

─────

'Travesti and I have long been bedfellows. He's my favourite wine writer. What he doesn't know about wine would have clothed the body of Charles the Bold when he was found on the battlefield."

"He was naked."

"Precisely."

─────

Hallyday's on holiday.
Will it be a jolly day
When Hallyday, on holiday,
Takes his umpteenth wife?
(Johnny Hallyday boasted of having gone to bed with many women. Would he not have valued staying with Nathalie Baye, the mother of his child?)

─────

Going home from the theatre, Nathalie Baye used to pass Truffaut's grave. He is for her "un absent présent".

─────

"My mother had a lot of ornaments; I only had a few; Greta has a lot; you tend to do the opposite of your parents."

─────

"Greta was surprised when I told her how much your father earned. I managed so well, she thought he had a good wage." She made budgets for other members of the family; I don't think they managed to keep to them.

─────

Bernd blinked his eyes a number of times.
"It's good exercise for the eyes," he said. He was anything but a blinking idiot. I saw a woman do that in the lower workshop at Donkin's.

─────

Bombay began as a city on islands, like Venice, yet unlike Venice.

─────

Her bath looked spartan, save for the yellow flowers at the foot. Does she imagine herself back in the eighteenth century when bathing? Would she have cared to be a mistress of Louis XV or would she have disdained such dependency? Boucher portraits could not have compared with her films. "She is beyond compare, on and off-screen." Pale yellow curtains—the colour of spirituality in India. Blue-painted walls—her taste seems fairly close to mine. My mother thought no two people have the same taste when decorating—in wallpaper, particularly. Her house is said to have a Proustian atmosphere; the courtyard has Moorish or Mogul echoes too. How many antique shawls has she? Is the oldest the most prized? Has she any Fortuny clothes? "She's eighteenth century in her bath, late nineteenth century in her sitting room and library, twentieth when filming, except that she's making historical films." Do shawls mean more to her than jewellery because they are soft and someone made them? "Lapidaries set and polish stones." When she wears a shawl, does she imagine the life of the seamstress who made it long ago? The hands have gone but the work of those hands remains.

Tapestry-covered chairs—are the tapestries antiques or new, made in the spirit of the late nineteenth century? A Chinese painting—does she see an affinity between late nineteenth century France and the Chinese art which intrigued Mallarmé and contemporary painters? Would she like to make a film with Zhang Yi-mou?

―――――

"It's back to Poland for me and back to the dole for you and backs to the wall for the country."

―――――

'They're funny when you're watching them," said my mother of Laurel and Hardy, "but they're funnier when you think about them afterwards."

―――――

My mother's father used to talk politics with the doctor. My father said it was impossible to tell which way they voted.

―――――

Months after Bernd went back to Germany, I was told by our landlady that the day his mother heard that his father had been killed on the Russian front his little brother was drowned in a brook at the bottom of the garden.

Chapter Nine

Lunch For The Projectionist

Olive liked taking lunch to her father at the cinema, where, from his little projectionist's room, he cast visions on the screen, like books come to life. She loved reading then. As the years went by, films appealed more and more, setting people she liked before her, intelligent men conversing, beautiful women, who, if they had gone naked, would at least have done it "with some style"—above all, perhaps, films were a reminder of her father, who was "a gentleman", very nice, and always ready to answer questions.

―――――

"A woman once said to me that Chanel number five is worn by loose women," said my mother. Did it give her a thrill to be, for once, in the company of loose women?

―――――

I liked the violin against Lata's voice. Is the nearest English equivalent to her timbre and the mood of such songs Emma Kirkby singing Dowland?

―――――

Do the fortresses of Rajasthan have reservoirs as well-appointed as those at Masada? If not, why not? Jodhpur after the monsoon looked drier than Greece or Sicily. It is an oasis on the edge of the Thar desert. Shortly before Diwali, nights are still hot enough for some people to sleep on roof-tops. There is not much piped water in Jodhpur; most people are dependent on age-old wells. Hanuman langhurs were allowed to steal fruit from a stall and waste water in a roof-top pitcher they broke. When one was electrocuted, it was treated like a human being, strewn with flowers, then cremated. The flowers were red and orange. How far north does the banyan tree grow? Does life revolve around the banyan tree?

―――――

They seemed to materialise out of the ground. Was the earth their element? Were there water-demons? Snow-demons, challenging the gods in their own fastness? Slippery without being wet, flickering without being light, fluorescent. She might have feared a form of magnetism, but that was beyond her. It was said that the heads of well-known politicians had floated in space, then turned in to a row of coconuts. Some put this down to hypnotism, others said the politicians had the brain of a coconut.

―――――

He was like a gushing oil well of a being, save that he only went up to seven feet or so; there was a face discernible in the oil; there were arms, or were there?

―――――

"It is said that Sinbad had to keep the kangaroo to himself because he knew no-one would believe him. He tucked it away in the pouch of his private memories."

―――――

Lunch For The Projectionist

Did Sinbad feel a greater attachment to the places where he had first heard of distant lands or to those lands themselves?

─────

It seemed ill-omened for Lakshmi Mittal to hold his daughter's wedding ceremony in Vaux-le-vicomte. Just after Nicolas Fouquet entertained Louis XIV there, he was imprisoned.

─────

The Indian leading man did a Harold Lloyd to the heroine, dropping garlands over her head one after another until there were twenty garlands pinning her arms to her sides and she could not move them, for fear of bursting the garlands.
    "I'm imprisoned in orange. Are you going to peel me?"

─────

'When I was trendy, I was wrong," said Tony. "God has more joy in my repentance than in all the good sense of conservatism, so I'm still one of God's elect and you can't argue with me."

─────

The two Blairs are blaring but the truth will out.

─────

The headmistress was a lady. Other teachers were nice but not ladies. It was an all-girls' school, separate from the neighbouring boys' school, but was there not a man among the teachers who each gave her pocket-money for the British Empire exhibition?

─────

My mother liked the name, Etienne, so "The Adventures of Gerard" would bring back happy memories.

―――――

Her two sisters and a brother had left the matchworks after a short time. "They used to say: "You like it there, don't you?" I didn't; but it was a job."

―――――

My mother used to hurry home to hear dance bands on the radio: Jack Hilton, Jack Parnell, Ambrose.

―――――

Sandra had donned her overcoat but was lingering in the cloakroom with break well advanced. As I took her arm, she admonished me defiantly:
"Stop loving me." I admired her timing.

―――――

"I'm always being caught with men in my room," bemoaned Katherine. "With some others it would mean something but I'm one of the most innocent people here."
She had hoped I had not heard ill of the hall of residence.
"It's supposed to be a school for young ladies."
On a later occasion, she said:
"I've always been the little girl of the group." But the group drank alcohol in pubs under-age. Besides going to church twice on Sundays, she was an inveterate partygoer.

―――――

Lunch For The Projectionist

'That lift takes seven minutes,' said Tom, the storeman, "so that's the one he uses."

'The floor's level here,' I pointed out, "and there aren't so many bends."

Helping him sort out components or load a trolley was the most congenial task, better than being outside in winter or being ordered about by four stupid supervisors, three of them women. (A big box of valves had to be moved from one side of the workshop to the other, then put back later in the day.) The store-room was peaceful and relatively warm. Tom liked Nana Mouscouri, I recall, and the most beautiful country he had seen was Japan. He had driven a library van which delivered to one school where a girls' cloakroom was beside the entrance, reached by a flight of steps. He claimed that the girls were in underclothes and went in to the showers, naked. I was able to inform him that it was my old school.

"We'll paint it red," one of the women told Tom cheerfully, letting him know the high jinks planned for Christmas Eve.

"What about Bryan's?"

"Bryan's too," she answered, enjoying my embarrassment. Were they going to give us the red mark of respect on the part of us they most respected?

Guru DLitt's "Pyaasa" has an upbeat ending: the poet is acclaimed and goes off with Gulab to seek happiness; the evil publisher and those he has bribed get their comeuppance. In "Kaagaz ke Phool", the film director declines in to drunkenness and comes back to die in his director's chair. One technician recognises him. The film was bound to be less popular. Did no-one see that coming? Guru Dutt lost confidence after his first flop. Alcohol must have brought on self-pity and despondency. He might have lived to see "Kaagaz ke

Phool" become a classic. Truffaut's "La Chambre Verte" was a flop on release, has won admirers since. Chabrol said cinema chains tried to prevent people from seeing it. The poet in "Pyaasa" (1957) is incarcerated in a mental hospital. Ezra Pound was released by the Americans next year. The screenplay is Dostoevskyan. I'd guess that Dostoevsky was Abrar Alvi's favourite novelist.

—————

"You reek of films," declared Roy.

—————

She wore a classic purple dress; not for her the vulgarity of excessive décolletée. Seemingly short when interviewed after the opening film, she looked taller on stage, announcing the awards. Isabelle looked startlingly youthful, her smile both sweet and slightly uncertain as she turned to the right, looking in to the wings, welcoming the prizewinner, her blue eyes putting jewels in their place. Her freshness was kept safe by intelligence and calm in the mill of commerce.

—————

Was my mother secretly complimented when I was attracted to dark-haired women, recalling her younger self?

—————

When people said children only like reading if there are many books in the house, my mother used to say:
'There weren't many books in our house but I loved reading."

—————

Lunch For The Projectionist

A strike cost my mother the house she liked at Armscote Close. Forever afterwards, she could not abide strikes.

―――――

There was a sound like a spoon vibrating against a cup yet I knew it was birdsong.

―――――

Spellbindingly beautiful as ever, she came and went in the labyrinth of tunnels like a comic angel. ("Subway")

―――――

"Home and Away" reminded me of the excitement of Germany when I was just sixteen. There is a sense of adolescents rising on a summer morning and going out to face a fresh, unsullied world. When I was in Brigitte's home that first morning in Germany, I had a sensation of the walls moving because I had been on a train so long. It only happened once for a moment.

(When it was patchy, some years before the vintage period which preceded its sad decline.)

―――――

I had Sophie in my eyes, prompting indulgent smiles.

―――――

I prefer Chloë's smile to Chloë.

―――――

'These ones or those ones?" These or those, Angel, if you want to be a writer.

—————

Katherine's face, without make-up, was heavy, as were her breasts in a white jumper.
   'Try Vick,' I suggested.
   "It would make my nose shiny," she replied, almost laughing, enjoying the intimacy between me and her nose. Was that a hint of how she felt a month later when she was sitting on a train, minding her own business, when four young men picked her up by the arms and legs and put her on a luggage-rack? Very chivalrous, the Yorkshire middle class.

—————

Richard and I had a sword-fight with Guardians (not my choice of paper). Roy, the political scientist, used to claim the papers to cut out articles, so he was puzzled and put out in the morning.

—————

Hogwood seemed to have taken the third Brandenburg Concerto a shade fast and at an even tempo, smoothing out the rhythm. A tune at the end should sound frantic and does when played with an accelerando in other performances.

—————

My mother loved the scent of white narcissi, did not care for that of geraniums.

—————

Lunch For The Projectionist

"I don't mind watching it when I know the result." Live tennis made her too excited.

———

"He's only twenty-one and he's good; he's going to be a great batsman," I said of Stephen Waugh. Happiness showed in my mother's eyes at my being happy.

———

On the beach with Kane, Jade looked French and reminded me of someone possibly not French. (Orane Demazis in the Pagnol trilogy?)

———

"Isn't she nice?" remarked my mother of Erica, the embroiderer. I agreed.

———

How many miles did it feel to the two mile umbrella? The endless distance of childhood or the light-footed bound of young limbs? Both in one? Did she think of the two mile umbrella as she walked in to Matlock on a sunny day? She used to descend the steep hill by the council offices instead of going down the Dimple as I did. Was that because she had done so when visiting my father convalescing in hospital in Matlock. Was he in the hospital not far from the council offices or the smaller one on the main road below Hackney—the one that had protected us from power-cuts the first winter at the cottage?

———

I had read of chucking in Dickens but never seen it. Ryan touched his sister under the chin as he broke off the conversation and walked past her.

Lara Cox can flush at will (as some actresses can cry at will). She is very fair-skinned and at moments of excitement her cheeks are flushed. It could hardly be done by applying make-up and removing it every few minutes. The effect is too subtle and, otherwise, she appears not to be made-up at all. Could a light be placed in such a position as to tinge both cheeks with rose without illuminating her whole figure in a ruddy glow?

When a sullen Ryan was bearded in his bedroom by Anita, she stood in the doorway, the main light coming from the landing. He kissed his sister on the cheek when under the influence of drugs. Has he done so at other times?

─────

Drazic had wanted to appear unconcerned but Anita's reaction to his unconcern concerned him. Anita wore black and plum as though part of her was in mourning for Drazic and part was not.

─────

That curvy Cervi's no scurvy Cervi.
Was she, at first, a nervy Cervi,
Wielding a brush as Artemisia
And trying to look the part of artist
And work of art in one? She shone as both.
What a rebellious pencil she had
But her soul shunned the soap-box:
Stridency does not make pictures.

─────

Lunch For The Projectionist

I tried to find a pound coin in my pocket, taking out a ten pence piece, and another, delving again—and producing the same two ten pence pieces, all the while feeling more exposed as she regarded me quizzically, mockingly, though not unsympathetically, and I ruefully tried to intimate that it was not my fault that I was ridiculous. Lucien Leeuwen must have felt a similar embarrassment when, for the second time, thrown from his horse below the window of a woman he sought to impress. Lucien was a good rider. I had better days.

—————

"I've always thought you should be in show business," said Roy.

—————

"You are an artist," observed Bernd as I tripped over a chair.

—————

Everybody's going to Thailand.
When will Thailand be my land?
The king of Siam is the great I am
As played by Yul Brynner, who made him a sinner.
Was he a spinner of history, Brynner?

—————

A vuvuzela from Venezuela
Is not so welcome as Uwe Seeler
Once was; it's as bad as a loudhailer.
Chavez thinks he's a Bob Marley Wailer
Yet has no more sense than a vuvuzela.

—————

The kickdonkey President has caused a furore in America, where donkeys are practising kicking, determined to get their retaliation in first and kick him to Kingdom Come.
"We'll bray him," said a Yorkshire-born donkey.

―――――

In a land of weasel words
What a boon is Özil,
Not so weighty as Musil
But with the grace of an ousel,
Sung by Shakespeare, sweeter than "Carousel".
And Liverpool did not choose the best tune.
"What's the use of wond'rin'" where the next manager takes you?
What's the use of trying to stop
Özil's flight of fancy?

―――――

Bernd won a box of chocolates at the International society for translating two sentences in to more languages than anyone else. I think his score was thirty-odd, not far off forty. He came back happy one night after talking to two French girls, who were in Leeds teaching. They were comfortable. He was still basking in the memory of their presence.

―――――

Ed Miliband assures us that he is Thoroughly Modern Millie.
　'Two Eds are not better than one. Their followers are known as Edy boys. It is feared that they will get out of hand in cinemas, dance in the aisles, tear up seats."

―――――

Lunch For The Projectionist

"Change! Change! God, I'm charismatic."

———

"A greengrocer said: "Buy your fruit where you buy your vegetables."
We grew our own vegetables. I had coupons."
(The Blitz spirit in Ilkeston.)

———

"Children of the sun,
Your time has just begun."
'That's you,' said my mother.

———

Lakshmi was proceeding under her own steam. Only a year earlier, she had been a babe-in-arms. She looked wide, as though wrapped in nearly as many layers as a Russian baby, swaddled against the cold by her babushka.